Hearing the Sermon

CHANNELS OF LISTENING

Believing in Preaching
Mary Alice Mulligan, Diane Turner-Sharazz,
Dawn Ottoni Wilhelm, Ronald J. Allen

Hearing the Sermon
Ronald J. Allen

Listening to Listeners
John S. McClure, Ronald J. Allen, Dale P. Andrews,
L. Susan Bond, Dan P. Moseley, G. Lee Ramsey Jr.

Make the Word Come Alive
Ronald J. Allen and Mary Alice Mulligan

Hearing the Sermon

RELATIONSHIP / CONTENT / FEELING

Ronald J. Allen

CHALICE
PRESS
ST. LOUIS, MISSOURI

Biblical quotations, unless otherwise noted, are from the *New Revised Standard Version Bible*, copyright 1989, Division of Christian Education of the National Council of the Churches of Christ in the United States of America. Used by permission. All rights reserved.

Scripture quotations marked (NIV) are taken from the HOLY BIBLE, NEW INTERNATIONAL VERSION®. NIV®. Copyright © 1973, 1978, 1984 by International Bible Society. Used by permission of Zondervan Publishing House. All rights reserved.

Cover art: © Getty Images
Cover and interior design: Elizabeth Wright

Visit Chalice Press on the World Wide Web at
www.chalicepress.com

10 9 8 7 6 5 4 3 2   06 07 08 09 10 11

Library of Congress Cataloging–in–Publication Data

Allen, Ronald J. (Ronald James), 1949-
  Hearing the sermon : relationship, content, feeling / Ronald J. Allen.
    p. cm.
  ISBN-13: 978-0-827205-01-7
  ISBN-10: 0-827205-01-5 (pbk. : alk. paper)
  1. Preaching–United States–Psychology–Case studies. 2. Listening–
Religious aspects–Christianity–Case studies. 3. Laity–United States–
Interviews. I. Title.

BV4235.L57A44 2004
251–dc22

2004011560

Contents

Preface

This book is based on interviews with people across a wide spectrum of ages, racial and ethnic identities, and denominations who listen to sermons. In 1999, the Lilly Endowment, located in Indianapolis, Indiana, agreed to support a study of such people through Christian Theological Seminary (Indianapolis). The study, which is described more fully in chapter 1, seeks to identify elements in preaching that engage and disengage congregations. The study team asked 263 lay people in twenty-eight congregations–some comprised mainly of African Americans, some comprised mainly of persons of non-Hispanic European origin, and some congregations that are racially and ethnically mixed–to become our teachers. We asked these folk, "Teach us how you listen to sermons so that we can help ministers become effective preachers." We also interviewed preachers in these congregations.

This volume is one of several that report findings from these extensive interviews. Each volume is distinct in that it reports the data from different points of view. Yet the different volumes work together as an informal series and are identified as such by the presence of a common logo on each volume.

- *Listening to Listeners: Homiletical Case Studies* (St. Louis: Chalice Press, 2004), by John S. McClure, Ronald J. Allen, Dale P. Andrews, L. Susan Bond, Dan P. Moseley, and G. Lee Ramsey, Jr., takes a case study approach by exploring in detail six interviews from the study and offering methods that pastors can use for interviewing their own congregations.
- The present book, *Hearing the Sermon: Relationship, Content, Feeling,* discusses the three main settings through which listeners process sermons: ethos (relationship), logos (content), and pathos (feeling).
- *Believing in Preaching: What Listeners Hear in Sermons,* by Mary Alice Mulligan, Dawn Ottoni Wilhelm, Diane Turner-Sharazz, and Ronald J. Allen, focuses on the pluralism of responses to specific questions and issues raised in the interviews. For example, this book reveals how listeners think God is active in the sermon.
- *Make the Word Come Alive: Lessons from Laity,* by Mary Alice Mulligan and Ronald J. Allen, summarizes principles for preaching that significant numbers of listeners report encourage them to want to pay attention to the sermon.

All these books rely extensively on the words and interpretive perspectives of the laity themselves.

We deeply thank the pastors and laity who participated in the study. They devoted much time and effort and were the epitome of grace and helpfulness. The pastors showed remarkable courage in allowing interviewers from outside the congregation to question parishioners about preaching. The listeners were sensitive, thoughtful, and candid.

For multiple forms of help while putting together this volume, I thank Mary Alice Mulligan, Associate Project Director, and the two Project Assistants who served during this time—Owen Cayton and Kara Brinkerhoff. I am also thankful to the people who did the actual interviewing: Dale P. Andrews, Bobbye Brown, Owen Cayton, Lisa Coffman, Lori Krase-Cayton, John S. McClure, Mary Alice Mulligan, G. Lee Ramsey, Jr., Edgar A. Towne, and Diane Turner-Sharazz. I further express appreciation to Melissa Green who patiently transcribed the interviews from tape recordings. The project team benefited much from the guidance of our consultant, Nancy Eiesland, Professor of the Sociology of Religion at Candler School of Theology at Emory University. We underline our gratitude to the leaders of Christian Theological Seminary who have supported this project: Edward L. Wheeler, President, as well as Deans who served during the conception and carrying out of this project (D. Newell Williams, Clark M. Williamson, and Carolyn M. Higginbotham). I am grateful to the Lilly Endowment who made this project possible, and especially two of the members of the Religion Division, Christopher Coble and Craig Dykstra. I express particular appreciation to the members of the Advisory Board who read and commented on an early draft of this book. In 1988 I dedicated *Preaching for Growth* (St Louis: CBP Press) to Genesis McKiernan-Allen, who was then five years of age. Now a twenty-year-old student at Lewis and Clark College, she spent a Christmas break reading this manuscript with a patient and discerning eye, and helping me avoid many infelicities. If the ideas in this volume eventually founder on the shoals of critical reflection and other research, these folk are not to blame.

Introduction

Most preachers have the experience of pronouncing the benediction at the end of a service of worship, walking to the rear of the sanctuary, and having some parishioners comment directly on the sermon at the door. Most say something like, "Nice sermon." Some listeners, however, either say a little more or make comments that prompt the preacher to want to know more about their responses.

After commenting on similarities between members of the congregation and the preacher that were revealed in a story from the preacher's own life told in the sermon, Ethel says, "You're one of us. One of us."[1] A preacher may naturally wonder why the theological concept at the heart of the sermon did not seem as important to Ethel as the fact that Ethel saw the preacher as "one of us."

Lorenzo, another parishioner, comments, "I am really interested in the big idea you developed in the sermon. Could you give me the title of a book that develops that idea more fully?" To be sure, the sermon may have been expressed in vivid language, been structured to create tension and drama, contained emotionally moving illustrations, and been spoken in a warm and engaging way in the pulpit. Yet Lorenzo was captivated by the idea at the heart of the sermon.

Still another person, Pat, comments on how moving the sermon was. "I was on the verge of tears. I even had to get my handkerchief and wipe my eyes. It was the story you told about God's love for us, even when we do things that are not loving. Sometimes I feel so unlovely, but your story made me feel loved." As the pastor at the door hearing such a remark, I have thought to myself, "That wasn't such a great story. Nor was this sermon any great shakes." Why would Pat respond with such emotion to a sermon that would have received, at best, a B-grade in preaching class in seminary?

1

I know from a lifetime of interaction with ministers that many preachers are interested in the fact that different people react differently to the same sermon. Indeed, some weeks different people react so differently to the sermon that I have wondered whether they all heard the same sermon.

Each Person Listens through a Distinct Setting

This book offers an interpretation of why these three listeners respond as they do, along with the many variations of these responses that are found in the typical congregation. An empirical study of people who regularly hear sermons called "Listening to Listeners" (see below) finds that different people listen to sermons on different *settings* that are within that person (and that are affected by external factors in the worlds of listeners).[2]

Because it is central to this book, the notion of "settings" needs to be clarified. Here the term "settings" does not refer to different geographical or social locations where preaching takes place (e.g., sanctuary, funeral home, or senior citizen residence). Instead, as noted above, these settings are within a person; a person listens to a sermon through one of these settings (and its distinct pattern of interaction with other settings). Factors that transcend the person (but are also tied to dynamics within the person) can influence a person's settings. Such a factor is congregational culture (discussed in chapter 1). Some aspects of a setting are self-conscious (and even critically considered), but some aspects (perhaps most) are unconscious, even intuitive.

A public address system used in many worship spaces provides an imperfect but useful analogy. The preacher speaks one sermon. The sermon goes through a microphone into a mixing console where amplification and mixing of the different qualities in the sound takes place. The console contains controls that the sound operator sets in order to influence the way the congregation hears the sermon. The settings on these controls can determine the volume and can highlight (or depress) other qualities in the voice that the congregation hears.

Everyone in the congregation hears the same sermon. But each person understands the sermon through that person's particular setting.[3] The three settings and their main themes are drawn from Aristotle. They are:

- ethos—which has to do with the congregation's perception of the character of the preacher and of their relationship with the preacher;
- logos—which has to do with the congregation's perception of the ideas of the sermon and with how the preacher develops those ideas;
- pathos—which focuses on the congregation's perception of the feelings stirred by the sermon.[4]

The study discovered that each person listens to the sermon through one of these settings—ethos, logos, or pathos—though the settings influence one another within each listener. Because each person's setting is different, and because the settings relate differently with one another within each person, I speak often in the plural of ethos settings, logos settings, and pathos settings.[5]

Figure 1 represents the analogy between the intermingling (or mixing) of ethos, logos, and pathos in the listener with the amplification and mixing of a speaker's voice in the sanctuary. The sermon is the input that goes into the mixing console. Ethos, logos, and pathos are the settings mixed within the self.[6] The settings are different for every parishioner. In some listeners, the ethos setting is mixed very high while logos and pathos are much lower, while in other hearers logos or pathos is mixed higher. In one congregant the ethos may be low, the logos mid-range, and the pathos very high, while in another the logos may be very high, the ethos mid-range, and the pathos almost turned off. Listeners hear some sermons very directly (as when the volume is turned up) but must strain to hear others (as when the volume is turned way down). The number of variations is limited only by the number of members in the listening community.

As noted previously, this analogy is imperfect. A mixing console is a mechanical device whose operations can be controlled and predicted, whereas the human being can respond to sermons (and other stimuli) in ways that are spontaneous and unexpected and that create unimagined possibilities.[8] However, the analogy does help us grasp what happens when people hear sermons.

For some people, such as Ethel, the character of (and relationship with) the preacher, and the qualities of the congregation as community, is the primary setting through which she hears the sermon. For others, represented by Lorenzo, the ideas in the sermon are more

Figure 1[7]

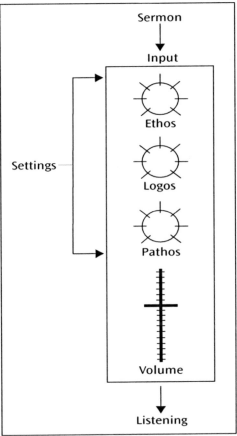

Mixing Console

basic, while for still others (like Pat) the feeling created by the sermon is the dominant setting.

While Ethel is usually most affected by the character of the preacher and by her sense of relationship with the minister, the ideas of a sermon can affect her and she can be moved emotionally by the sermon. For Ethel, the character of the preacher is somewhat more important than the ideas (as ideas) of the message, or the degree to which she is touched emotionally. If she neither respects the preacher as a person nor feels a sense of relationship, she tends to discount the other aspects of preaching (though not dismissing them completely). A different pattern of response is true for Lorenzo who pays most attention to a sermon with compelling ideas, but who can be affected by awareness of the preacher's character and can also be moved emotionally. Pat is most attuned to the sermon through the ways it touches her emotionally. She certainly responds to ideas and the character of the preacher but they often seem most compelling to her when they stir feelings.

Chapter 1 describes how the idea came about that a person typically listens to a sermon through a primary setting: ethos, logos, or pathos. Chapter 2 explores the ethos setting, and comments on some of its interactions with the other two settings. Chapter 3 focuses on the logos setting, and its relationship with ethos and pathos. Chapter 4 moves to the pathos setting and its interaction with ethos and logos. Chapter 5 reflects theologically on this typology, and considers how to work with the three different settings in particular sermons. Chapter 6 is an example of moving from thinking about a sermon on Luke 3:7–18 in a particular congregation to the completed sermon. Appendix A contains the questions asked in the interviews. Appendix B contains a table comparing key elements of the three settings for listening to sermons. Appendix C is a list of typical expressions used by persons in each of the three settings.

CHAPTER 1

Three Settings through Which People Hear Sermons

Since my ministry now takes place in a theological seminary and I no longer preach every week in a congregation, I often sit in the sanctuary of the congregation where our household attends. My experience of the service is affected by the ways in which the sound system is set. When the sound system is adjusted to the speaker's voice, I can hear and easily follow the sermon and the service. When the sound is too low, I have difficulty hearing, and my attention wanders. Once in a while the sound system in the congregation where I worship squawks and at other times picks up communications from police cars and other vehicles in the neighborhood who are communicating with two-way radios. The settings of the sound system, and the things the system picks up (and does not pick up), go a long way towards shaping how I experience the service and what I take home.

In a similar way, interviews with 263 people who regularly listen to sermons reveal that a listener typically hears a sermon through one of three settings that affect how the listener perceives the message: ethos, logos, or pathos.[1] Ethos is perception of the character of (and relationship with) the preacher; logos refers to the content of the sermon and how the preacher develops it; pathos bespeaks feelings generated by the sermon and how they orient (or disorient) the listener towards the sermon.

It is important to note that a listener does not usually hear the sermon only as an event of ethos, logos, or pathos. All three qualities are at work within every person who hears sermons, and they interact with one another in different ways in each listener.[2] A person who listens through an ethos setting, for instance, is still affected by logos and pathos. The ethos setting brings ethos qualities to the fore while logos and pathos modes of perception continue to operate. Furthermore, these settings function differently in each listener. In one person, just as the adjustments on the bass range may be so strong as to overpower the tenor range, so the adjustments on the ethos setting may be so high that the listener is barely aware of the logos and pathos elements of sermons, while in another listener the ethos setting may be only slightly more prominent than logos or pathos. Such variations can also be true for the person who listens on pathos settings.[3]

In this chapter, I first review the broad lines of the study and how ethos, logos, and pathos function as settings through which people perceive the sermon. The heart of the chapter reflects on how we can recognize the setting through which a listener perceives the sermon, and how the different perspectives interact with one another in a single listener. Along the way, cautions are raised about oversimplifying the listening dynamics within a congregant or a community as well as to reflect theologically on listener preferences.

We Asked People to Teach Us How They Listen to Sermons

I had a surprising recognition a few years ago. Although sermons are prepared for laity (and other listeners), very few preachers or people who write about preaching ask listeners what helps the listeners pay attention to a sermon (and what puts them off). Most books on preaching that suggest what makes a sermon "work" depend on biblical theology, systematic theology, philosophy of language, studies in orality and aurality, as well as literary criticism, speech communication theory, rhetoric, or the writer's personal experience as a preacher. To be sure, the literature of preaching in the last decade speaks of a "turn to the listener," yet few preachers or writers in the field of preaching have asked large numbers of folk who hear sermons to indicate qualities in sermons that engage them and qualities that allow their attention to drift away.[4]

At the turn of the twenty-first century, a study, called "Listening to Listeners," sponsored by the Lilly Endowment through Christian Theological Seminary, undertook such an exploration.[5] This project, advised by a group of eight recognized scholars of preaching, interviewed more than 260 laity who regularly hear sermons in twenty-eight congregations to teach us how they listen.[6]

Since the time of Aristotle, people who study human communication between a speaker and an audience have recognized key dynamics at work: the audience's perception of the person and character of the preacher (ethos), the audience's perception that the speaker has developed the content of the sermon to show that the message of the speech is true (logos), and the audience's response to the feelings and identifications generated in connection with the sermon (pathos).[7] While not identified by Aristotle as one of the essential aspects of preaching, our project advisory board also identified embodiment (or delivery), as an important aspect of preaching. We asked the individuals and small groups several questions about each of these settings (ethos, logos, pathos, and embodiment).[8] In the process, we gathered a lot of information not only about how each setting functions in a listener and a congregation, but about how the different settings interact with one another.[9]

Because frequent reference is made to the interview questions in the rest of the book, the questions are listed in appendix A in the categories in which they were asked. I discuss the categories themselves and summarize what we learned from the interviews in separate chapters: ethos in chapter 2, logos in chapter 3, and pathos in chapter 4.

Quotes from the Transcripts

In the materials that follow, I try to let the people who were interviewed in the study speak for themselves. That is, instead of simply offering my own summaries of listener remarks, I quote extensively from the transcripts themselves so that the reader can both hear the listeners in their own words and reflect critically on the interpretations offered here.[10] I typically select individual quotes that represent several other quotes in the body of interviews and indicate this representative quality by introductory words such as "Many listeners say." I also indicate when a quote is found in only a few transcripts.

Information such as gender, age, racial and ethnic identity, size and geographical setting of the congregation is given only when it seems pertinent to a particular listener's comment. Usually I refer to interviewees by generic expressions such as "a listener in the study," or "another person who hears sermons." To this point in our work with the interviews, we have found the general patterns in the descriptions of the three different settings articulated in this book to be about equally distributed in actual listeners in the study population. Further analysis of the transcripts may reveal nuances of difference between women and men, different age groups, and the various racial and ethnic communities.

Since we promised anonymity to interviewees, any material in the interview that could identify a congregation, city, or person has been omitted. When necessary to understand a particular comment, I provide a sense of the context of the interview in which the comment occurs.

Most of the listeners' remarks quoted herein are straightforward. The quotes that I have selected are consistent with other things that each congregant says in the interview. Furthermore, readers will find that many of the remarks quoted from the transcripts manifest qualities often associated with oral expression, such as repetition, broken speech, expressions that appear awkward in print, sentence fragments, and grammar that differs from recommendations in conventional textbooks of English grammar. Insofar as possible, I have left the words of the interviewees as they were spoken. I have slightly edited a few such quotes in this book for ease in reading and to help maintain the anonymity of the interviewees. I have, for instance, removed pronouns such as "he" or "she" and replaced them with designations such as "the pastor" or "God" (except when gender reference is important to understanding the quote). Sometimes I supply a phrase that clarifies a listener comment within a quote or modify listeners' remarks slightly for clarity with square brackets [like this].

Most People Listen through One Setting

Having reviewed the broad lines of the study, it is time to overview one of the major discoveries, how it came to light, and how it helps us understand listening. When the interviews were completed, the project team began to look carefully at the transcripts of the interviews. We expected two things, both of which had to be revised.

First, we expected that the interviewees would respond to questions in relatively straightforward ways. When asked a question about ethos, for instance, we expected them to give a direct answer that illumines how ethos functions for them when they hear a sermon. Often, this very thing occurred. However, when asked about one category, some interviewees occasionally responded with information about another category. When asked a question designed to elicit the listener perspective about logos, a respondent might speak in terms of pathos. When asked about pathos, a listener might give an ethos response.

Second, we anticipated that each setting would function with approximately the same degree of force in each listener. To be sure, we thought that different listeners would be affected in slightly different degrees by ethos, logos, and pathos, but that the variations would be small.

We puzzled initially over what to make of the fact that some listeners respond to a question about one category with material from another. In a breakthrough moment Mary Alice Mulligan, associate director for the project (as well as director of the chapel and visiting professor of preaching and ethics at Christian Theological Seminary) hypothesized that, regardless of the question we asked, such hearers were revealing the aspect of listening that functions most prominently for them. "In a sense," she said, "they may be telling us, even unconsciously, what they most want us to know about what is important to them when they hear preaching. The person who gives us a pathos response when we ask an ethos or logos question may signal us that the experience of pathos is really what makes a sermon a sermon for them."

We reviewed dozens of transcripts with an eye toward confirming or disconfirming Professor Mulligan's hypothesis, and found that they point to a phenomenon that is key to this book: nearly every listener reveals that one setting is the mode through which they listen to the sermon.[11] At the same time, we need to keep in mind the fact that the hearer not only listens to the sermon through that primary setting but that the listener is also processing material received on the other settings and that the settings affect one another. To draw another analogy from the world of technology, the listener is always "mixing" the various responses to the sermon.

Our review of the transcripts finds that listeners reveal the setting on which they begin to listen to the sermon in three ways.[12] First, in responding to a question, some listeners state their primary listening setting directly.[13] For example, one reveals that this person's listening begins with logos. The interviewer asks, "Have you ever heard a sermon that just left you cold?"

> No. I try to be really open and receptive. When I sit down, my premise in life is I want to learn something everyday. So I'm going to listen. I'm hopefully going to be engaged, and I'm not going to walk out like, "What just happened?"

A moment later, the respondent continues:

> I take the sermon as a vehicle to learn. I am opening myself up to be taught something that maybe I don't know. Or it is allowing me to see it differently...I come to hear about what we have in this book of God's teaching. So how do we take those teachings and make them applicable to what's going on everyday?

This listener's logos orientation comes out with particular force in response to the inquiry, "What do you think God is doing in the sermon itself?"

> I think God is looking down saying, "How are you all receiving this? How are you all dealing with this? Who's listening? Who's not listening? Who's paying attention? Who's going to walk out and do something?"

Similar logos themes permeate the interview. Indeed, when asked about her high points and low points in listening to sermons, this listener replies, "I guess I don't look at it as having any low points. I mean I learn something from every Sunday, whether I want to or not."

Second, others disclose their entry-point setting in the way discussed above–by responding to a question about one category through material that relates to another category. A question probing for pathos was put to a listener, "Can you think of a sermon that you found particularly stirring?"

> Not really, because I usually find something in most sermons. Reverend [pastor's name], one of the things I like about...I love Reverend [name], but I love all ministers. They have to be doing some terrible things for me not to like them. I was raised to do

this, and it became a part of me, part of my life, part of my being. I'm explaining why I love Reverend [name]. First, this pastor loves people. The pastor is always telling them. The pastor lets them know the pastor loves them. The pastor usually says, "If you don't like me to love you, there's nothing you can do about that." The minister is on a trip. So that opens the door when you know somebody really loves you and cares for how you are. It brings you closer to the minister, because if the minister stands away and just shakes your hand, "How are you doing today?" Well, it's just a form you go through, but this minister doesn't let you do that.

Although the question asked about pathos, the parishioner answered in almost purely ethos terms. When we read the transcript from start to finish, it became clear that relationship is central not only to the listener's perception of the preacher and the sermon, but in this listener's broader theological world view and in what this listener values in the congregation itself. Indeed, the hearer's primary logos concern is for how the sermon can help this person relate positively with God, with the people in the congregation, and in the world.

Third, most listeners reveal their base setting by returning to it repeatedly in the interview and by speaking about that setting in ways that indicate its function.[14] Many listeners leave clues that reveal the setting that is their window into the sermon. Such clues differ from person to person but often include the intensity of response to certain questions, the recurrence of key themes throughout the interview, and the amount of time they devote to certain subjects.

For instance, a hearer leaves a pattern of remarks that reveal this person's pathos orientation. This congregant explains that one of the values of preaching is "having an opportunity to look at a passage of scripture through the eyes of the preacher" because, among other things, the preacher helps the congregation see aspects of the cultural setting of the Bible that are different from today's world. "Of course, I do this all the time anyway in my own teaching at a university." When the interviewer asks, "What is your field?" the interviewee names the field and says:

> …but it's the same. I run into the same thing trying to explain why this poem [in the culture in which this person teaches] means what it did in the time period. It's not just words on a page. It's actually an expression of emotion, stimulated by some kind of event. I feel the same way about a biblical text, and that's what the sermon function is.

Several times in the interview, as in the following remark, this respondent says that some sermons make him "squirm," that is, feel self-conscious or uncomfortable. Squirming, a visceral reaction to the sermon, is a pathos motif. The notion of squirming as well as a broader statement about pathos as the beginning point for this listener emerges after the question, "What do you think God is doing during the sermon?"

> Hmmm…I think basically what God is doing is God's in between us in the sermon. I think it's God that makes us squirm. God's the one that touches us. It's in the words, yes, but it's, I guess the Holy Spirit's in the language and in the sermon itself, and that's what we're reacting to. It's not just the words. It's an emotional reaction. That's what's generating it. It's not, I don't think, anything else.

For this listener, God is something like an emotional presence that is in the congregation and that generates the congregation's feeling in response to the sermon. Not surprisingly, this interviewee remembers the emotional effects of a sermon but not the content.

> I cannot think of a single sermon that I think of as memorable enough to remember. I may want to go back and read it over again, but never reach the point where one so affected me that I was able to remember it for a long time. I can remember the effect, but I can't remember exactly what it was that the sermon was about.

When asked to recall some of the effects, this person continues in overtly pathos terms:

> I can think of times when I was uplifted. I can think of times when I cried. I can think of times when I felt uncomfortable, times when I was inspired. But what inspired me, I don't know. What the meat of the sermon was, I don't know.

In the interview as a whole, this listener expresses real appreciation for logos concerns (a clear message that makes sense and that deals with important matters), but for this hearer, logos leads to pathos.

The Settings Interact with One Another

Even more significant for understanding listening, as we read the transcripts it became apparent that one setting was not just more important than others, but that the listener tends to process the others through the perspective through which they listen to the sermon. For some listeners, ethos is the setting through which the listener usually receives logos and pathos. A sense of relationship with (and respect for) the preacher enables them to take seriously the content of the sermon; they *feel* (pathos) connected to the preacher and the sermon. For others, logos is the wavelength through which much ethos and pathos pass as they operate in the self. For still others, of course, pathos is the band through which the listener processes logos and ethos.[15]

The exact make-up of these interactions differs from person to person. One person whose base frequency is the logos setting may place a high priority on ethos concerns, but very little on pathos. Such a person might even say (as one interviewee does), "I am not an emotional person when it comes to sermons."[16] Another member who tunes into the sermon on the logos setting might give less importance to ethos and more to pathos. Several of our interviewees say, flatly, "I do not even have to like the preacher to get something out of the sermon."

The interaction of the different settings can be represented by means of a graph.[17] Dale P. Andrews, a distinguished teacher of preaching at Louisville Presbyterian Theological Seminary, suggests a simple graph with two perpendicular axes and four quadrants to represent the setting through which a listener begins to process the sermon.[18] In figure 2, each quadrant represents a different setting: ethos; logos; pathos, embodiment.[19] The setting through which the parishioner initially receives the sermon is plotted in that quadrant. The rays extend from that point to show the relative degrees of relationship of the interaction of the settings in the listener. The rays can be narrowed or widened to show the relationship. Figure 2 helps us visualize how the settings interact in the next interviewee discussed (immediately below) who begins listening on the logos setting and for whom pathos is the most important secondary setting, but for whom ethos and embodiment also play a role.

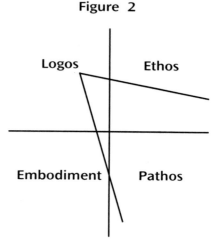

Figure 2

Logos   Ethos

Embodiment   Pathos

Similar graphs can be made for the person who synthesizes the sermon through the ethos setting and the pathos setting. In those cases, however, the rays initiate in the quadrant designating that setting.

We can observe the settings interacting with one another in the following excerpts from transcripts. An interviewee was asked a question designed to elicit how she understands pathos to function when she hears a sermon. "Can you tell me about a sermon that stirred your own emotions?" This person replied:

> I guess the ones that have made me think the most are when the senior minister does these sorts of dialogue sessions.[20] There was this one in particular...I saw the pastor the next day at a committee meeting. I said, "You were on fire yesterday." The senior minister

said, "Oh, I'm so glad to hear that, because I didn't really feel like I was on that day." But I guess when the senior minister challenges me to think, to understand better the roots of our scripture (and the senior minister does that in Bible study sessions as well), this minister just really causes you to think."

When asked to reflect on what stirs her emotions in preaching (pathos), the interviewee gave a logos response, "I guess the ones that have made me think..."

The parishioner's remark further illustrates the complicated interplay that can take place between logos and pathos. This response does contain a pathos element ("You were on fire yesterday"). The listener felt fire. However, the fire was activated because the preacher challenged this listener to think, "to understand better the roots of our scripture." Challenging *ideas* (logos) set this congregant on fire, i.e., set off an emotional response (pathos).

A review of the transcript of the interview reveals that this listener consistently interprets the sermon from a logos perspective. Logos even activates her ethos perceptions. Ethos, logos, and pathos are all present and important to this congregant, but logos is the primary setting through which the hearer processes ethos and pathos. Ethos and pathos elements in the sermon are typically important to this person as they relate to the logos setting.

Another person in one of the congregations in the study was also asked, "Can you think of a sermon that has stirred the congregation's emotions? If so, what happened after that?"

As I was relating before, we had a pastor that was very good at unifying. This pastor had the traits of a leader. I think it would have served the pastor well in the secular world had the pastor been a manager in human resources at a large corporation, or if the pastor had been superintendent of schools in the local school district. This pastor just had a charisma and a means of making you want to get on board with where the pastor was going and believe in what the pastor was all about. I think that's rare. I've also listened to sermons from folks who didn't have a quality of personality that draws people to them. They may have everything a good speaker needs, except the personality to make you want to be engaged in where they're going.

Although asked about preaching and emotion, the parishioner instead brings up the qualities of the preacher as person and leader. This focus on ethos recurs throughout the interview, as in the following reply to the question, "Can you think of a specific instance in which that pastor [the one mentioned in the quote above] preached a sermon, and the congregation seemed to be stirred?"

Yes. The pastor was calling on us as a congregation to get on board to start to plan for a church expansion that we didn't feel we needed yet, as far as building-wise. As far as people in the church, we were at about 80 percent capacity, and yet the pastor shared that according to statistics that are gathered by churches and church planners, when you get to that point, you really need to start looking at the next level, because you never will get to 100 percent and maintain that congregation. People will start to get dissatisfied with being crowded, or being too far, or the acoustics aren't correct so you'll regress. The pastor talked about the vision he had and invited us to be a part of that vision. The pastor talked about the scripture that begins, "If my people who were called by God's name." When the pastor shared, first the pastor gave the statistical or analytical vision. Then the pastor laced it with the biblical perspective of stepping out on faith. Even though it would have been a step of faith to encourage us to step to that place with the pastor, and the fact that the pastor was vested in the community at that time. It wasn't someone who had come in two years earlier. In the back of my mind, with a person like that, you might wonder, "We're all going to step out, and where will you be? Will you be with us in five years?" So the pastor was a very vested part of the community. The pastor had displayed commitment to the community and that church for a number of years, so the pastor was believable.

When asked about a sermon that stirred the congregation, the respondent speaks about the preacher having facts straight about the relationship between the capacity of the worship space, attendance and who manifests the integrity of commitment to the community.

But, when push comes to shove, this listener begins to process the sermon from the perspective of ethos. When the preacher has integrity, this listener will take the content (logos) seriously. We learn at another point in the interview, however, that if the preacher lacks integrity, this listener tunes out and does not pay attention to the ideas of the sermon "even when they may be true."

When asked about a sermon that caused another listener to think or act differently (a logos question), a parishioner said:

When you come into a sermon, probably each sermon should make you think in some way because God's word always gives you a different revelation. See? If God's word doesn't touch you, then something's wrong with you. So I could probably say that mostly they all kind of touched me, but I don't remember what the sermon was about [though the listener has some recollection that it was about God lifting your burdens]...Something about that sermon just made me fill up, and I went downstairs, and tears started coming to my eyes going downstairs. My burdens came out. Sermons all touch you some way to me.

For this person, the sermon does have an intellectual component, but a good sermon "touches" you. A main purpose of logos is to touch pathos. Indeed, the interview as a whole reveals that this listener tunes into the sermon on the pathos setting. The logos of the sermon (evidently the reminder that God helps us with our burdens) set off a pathos response (the listener felt burdens lifted).

Another interviewer posed this query to another interviewee. "Can you describe a time for me when the sermon stirred emotions or seemed to move the congregation?"

Yes. I think that happens very frequently where the congregation gets into the spirit of what the minister's trying to explain. It's like you get into any kind of gathering where everybody seems to be going along or inspired by the same thing. I think there's an emotional high that occurs. Sometimes in sports it's when someone does an exciting or unusual physical feat, but I think sometimes you can get the same type of feeling from an intellectual feat.

Although the question asks for the congregant to reflect on the role of pathos in listening, the congregant frames the response in terms of logos: the congregation "gets into the spirit" on the basis of what the preacher explains. From the perspective of the whole interview, these words are a clue that this person enters the sermon on the logos setting. This congregant wants the preacher to explain the Bible and Christian faith. The person experiences an emotional high because the sermon performs the significant logos function of explanation.

Remarks on Embodiment Vary Little from Setting to Setting

The listeners' remarks on embodiment vary little from one setting to another. The team analyzing the transcripts has found only one consistent correlation between a particular setting and a particular style of embodying the sermon.[21] The interviewees' remarks about embodiment give us the largest cluster of closely related ideas in the study:

- These folk like to be able to hear the preacher easily.
- They want to see the preacher.
- Eye contact gives many of them a feeling of connection with the preacher.
- Their interest in the sermon rises when the preacher uses expressive tones of voice (and they lose interest when the preacher speaks in monotone).

- They hope the preacher will show some life and energy in the pulpit. The amount of life and energy they like varies from person to person and congregation.
- They want to sense that the preacher is warm and fully present with the congregation.
- They are most comfortable when they see that the preacher is comfortable in the pulpit.
- They are energized when they feel that the preacher cares about them and the subject of the sermon. They like to feel the preacher's passion, though, of course, different persons and congregations recognize and appreciate different modes whereby passion is expressed.
- They are drawn to preachers who speak and act in the pulpit in ways that are consistent with how the preachers speak and act the rest of the week.

The people in our interview group say they are discouraged from listening when they cannot hear or see the preacher, when the preacher is stiff and lifeless in the pulpit, and when the preacher is uncomfortable.

Members of the study group exhibit considerable variation within these inclinations.[22] Some listeners prefer more energetic and louder embodiment, while others prefer more gentle and quiet styles. One listener interprets shouting in the pulpit as a positive demonstration of passion while another resents relentless shouting. Some listeners like for the preacher to stay behind the pulpit while others are drawn to preachers who leave the pulpit and move around the worship space while preaching. However, except for a correlation between a particular aspect of embodiment and pathos (discussed in chapter 4), I cannot see that such differences in response are associated with particular settings.[23]

Of course, there are voices from all three settings who qualify or even run against these preferences. A handful of listeners say they do not need to see the preacher. However, again, such variations are not associated with particular listener settings.

In the chapters on ethos, logos, and pathos settings, I mention embodiment only when it seems directly pertinent to persons who hear the sermon through the setting being discussed.

Many Themes Found in Listeners on All Settings

The presence of an isolated remark in a particular transcript does not mean that the listener hears the sermon through the setting typically associated with that remark. Similar remarks about many subjects can be found in some transcripts in all three settings. We find comments associated with ethos in transcripts that are oriented towards logos and pathos settings. Similarly, we find listeners referring to qualities of hearing that we associate with logos in interviews that reveal overall ethos or pathos settings, while qualities that sometimes signal pathos settings appear in interviews that lean towards logos and ethos. For example, persons who attend to the sermon on ethos, logos, and pathos settings all mention that their attentiveness to the sermon is affected by their perception of the integrity of the preacher. Congregants who hear through ethos settings tend to place more importance on integrity than do congregants who receive the sermon through logos or pathos.

As we have noted earlier, this phenomenon points to the complexity of listening and to the fact that a listener can never be reduced to a single setting. The dials and gauges of a sound system allow for considerable "mixing" of the different qualities of sound. Similarly, listening characteristics mix differently in each listener. The designations of ethos settings, logos settings, and pathos settings point to distinct patterns, but the patterns are not exclusive. Qualities associated with different settings interact with one another.

Pre-publication Review: Naming What We Observe

The main ideas of this study were tested at a public conference at Christian Theological Seminary before they were solidified for publication. The people interviewed in the study—laity and preachers—were invited not only to hear the major themes in our analysis of ethos, logos, and pathos, but to reflect on the degree to which these ideas seemed true to their experiences as listeners and preachers. A general invitation was also given to pastors and laity in the study area.[24]

In small groups and in plenary session, these people generally reported that the broad lines of interpretation unfolded in this book seemed to explain to the laity how they listen and seemed to help explain to the preachers what they observe among the congregations who hear their sermons. Several of the pastors at the conference, and pastors with whom we have informally discussed some of these ideas in other settings, said that the way we have explained ethos, logos, and pathos as settings through which people respond to sermons gave them a way of naming and talking about things that they observe in congregations.

This book is an even more public test of not only general vectors of our modest reinterpretation of the functions of ethos, logos, and pathos, but also of many more specific insights that have not been aired previously. We hope that the more detailed perspectives prove helpful to preachers who, week by week, seek to witness faithfully to the gospel through the sermon. We also hope that a broadly based, thoughtful conversation will ensue in which the positive findings of this study can be amplified and refined, and its weaknesses considered.

In the next chapters we turn to more detailed discussion of the settings of ethos, logos, and pathos. What are the characteristics of listening in each setting? How do they interact? What can the preacher do to appeal to the listener on each setting?

CHAPTER 2

Ethos Settings

In the Introduction, we encountered Ethel, a listener who, after hearing a story in a message that surfaced similarities between members of the congregation and the preacher, prompted Ethel to respond to the sermon, "You're one of us. One of us." For Ethel, the awareness that the minister is "one of us" not only functions to establish the credibility of the preacher and, hence, of the claims of the message (as in traditional rhetoric), but is itself a key part of the experience of hearing the sermon. For Ethel, the sermon is a means of relationship with the preacher.

Ethel's perspective is shared by many other people. The study behind this book discovered that many persons who listen to the sermon through ethos settings are concerned not only with the character of the preacher, but also think of preaching as a relationship with the pastor and even see the purposes of preaching as encouraging relationships. Such listeners most fully feel that they have heard a sermon when they feel a sense of relationship with the preacher and with other people in the congregation.

In this chapter, I first outline the characteristics of ethos in rhetoric and how the category of congregational culture comes into an expanded notion of ethos. The core of the chapter is turning to the transcripts from our interviewees to listen to persons who listen to the sermon on ethos settings describe how they experience preaching. The chapter then considers ways in which listeners on ethos settings interact with logos and pathos material. In connection with the different discussions in the chapter, I note things a preacher can do to enhance appeal to the person who hears the sermon through ethos.

Characteristics of Ethos in Rhetoric

For Aristotle, and many in the tradition of classical rhetoric, ethos refers to how the hearer's perception of the character of the speaker influences the hearer's receptivity to the message. From this point of view, a public speaker "persuades by moral character" by delivering a public address "in such a manner as to render" the speaker "worthy of confidence."[1] How a congregation (or other audience) perceives the character of a rhetor (speaker) affects their receptivity to the claims the rhetor makes in the public communication. The more confidence folk have in the speaker as a person, the more seriously they are willing to take the message.

Lucy Lind Hogan and Robert Reid, leading scholars who interpret the significance of rhetoric for preaching, point out that one dimension of ethos is within the sermon itself, i.e., internal ethos. While embodying the sermon, the preacher can say and do things that reinforce the congregation's sense of trust in the preacher and in the message. The preacher seeks to create a persona in the pulpit that will "leave the listeners favorably disposed to listening to and agreeing with" the preacher.[2] Some of the things that a preacher can do within the message to enhance trust include representing the congregation's values and best interests, and demonstrating respect for the congregation, both in the content of the words spoken as well as in the way the sermon is embodied.[3]

Things that happen outside the event of preaching itself, i.e., external ethos (external to the sermon), can also contribute to the congregation's willingness to receive the sermon in a favorable way. Some things that contribute to external ethos include the following: the congregation's perception that the preacher lives in a way that is consistent with what the preacher says, that the preacher thinks sensitively and meaningfully about life, that the preacher has the requisite credentials from the church and other authorizing bodies, and that the preacher has a pleasing appearance.[4] David Cunningham, a systematic theologian who explores the importance of rhetoric for theology, speaks of the following additional dimensions of external ethos, which he calls "collateral information": the groups and people with whom the preacher associates (especially people and groups whom the congregation respects), evaluative remarks made by others about the preacher, details of the speaker's life that enhance credibility, previous familiarity with the preacher's speaking skill, and personal contacts with the preacher that leave a positive effect.[5]

A listening community often distrusts a speaker when they think the speaker is affiliated with groups they distrust, keeps herself or himself distant from the community, repeatedly criticizes the listeners, or whose way of living goes against the content of what the preacher says in sermons.

In the best situation, the way the congregation perceives the preacher is the way the preacher is in real life. When a congregation discovers discontinuity between their positive perception of the preacher and the preacher's actual life, they often lose confidence in the preaching. For that matter, a preacher's indiscretion in leadership far removed from preaching may cause some in the congregation to pay less attention to the sermons.

Congregational Culture and Ethos

Rhetoric in antiquity tended to concentrate on individual speeches given for specific purposes. Preaching, by contrast, takes place in a particular community over a long period of time. Indeed, some ministers can preach in fairly stable communities for many years. Over the past twenty years, the discipline known as congregational studies has helped us realize that each congregation is a particular culture with its own values, practices, and expectations.[6] A community's apprehension of the pastor and the message is influenced by the culture within the congregation.

Some readers may think that the connection between ethos and congregational culture is tenuous. However, two points suggest these categories are closely related. The first is that external ethos often involves qualities that arise from the life of the congregation. One could almost see congregational culture as a subcategory of external ethos. However, a difference of emphasis between external ethos and congregational culture is that the latter necessarily implies a communal dimension, whereas the broader category of external ethos includes phenomena that are associated with individual listeners as individuals. Congregational culture calls attention to aspects of ethos that arise from the congregational system.[7]

The second point of connection between ethos and congregational culture is that many people who hear sermons on ethos wavelengths regard their perception of the preacher and the sermon as representative of the congregation as community. The relationship between the preacher and the congregation at the time of the sermon is a kind of model of the relationship between preacher and people in the broader life of the church. For example, one congregant reports listening to a sermon with two ears— one focused on getting "personal direction for my life. Then, of course, I always have that second ear that I'm listening to see, 'Does this sermon represent who I think our church is?...Is this the kind of church that I'm inviting people to, and how are we doing in that way, too [that is, are we as a church living out the message that the preacher is giving]?'"

For example, some congregations have a tradition of expecting "great preaching;" in such a congregation, the simple fact of the preacher standing up to preach evokes a high level of credibility and a strong sense of expectation. Even in a congregation with a tradition of great preaching, the preacher can fritter away the respect of the congregation. Congregational expectations can be quite long lasting. In congregations with the expectation of great preaching, however, the congregation's perception that one pastor's preaching is ineffective seldom alters the tradition. The congregation expects the next minister to be a great preacher and brings that positive anticipation to the sermon.

It is important to note, of course, that the preacher and the sermon affect congregational culture and the ways that the congregation perceives the preacher and the sermon. The ways in which the sermon speaks within, to, and about the congregation affects the congregation's self-perception and can lead the congregation to expect (or not expect) certain things of the sermon.

Many congregants pointedly say the preacher needs to speak with the congregation in its particularity. When asked for one or two things a listener would want to tell preachers, one interviewee said, "Get to know your congregation. I think the more intimate level you the preacher are on with a congregation, the more apt they're going to be to take whatever you say or feel." Another person remarks:

> Sometimes the minister is just reading off the page, off the book, or it's just something they could've downloaded off the internet or copied from a book. Or maybe somebody gave them that sermon. They kind of read it to us. Then I tend to get bored and not pay as close attention. I try sometimes, but it seems like my mind wanders more if it's just kind of being read to me and it's not even relating to our church or particular people personally.[8]

Another hearer perceptively finds that the concern for preaching to be particular to particular congregations is not simply a matter of adapting to the audience, but is grounded theologically. "God knows each specific congregation and what they need to be uplifted and what they need to be better Christians." The preacher should do the same.

While a preacher needs to respect the particularity of the congregation, the preacher needs also to remember that congregational culture is never theologically neutral (and can never be theologically pure). A congregation may nurture values and practices that reflect the gospel, but a congregation may also encourage attitudes and actions that contradict the core values of Christian tradition. The preacher is to think critically with the congregation about ways congregational culture is consistent with the gospel and points at which the congregation needs to reformulate its culture to become more faithful.[9] A pastor hopes to do so in ways that maintain positive ethos so that the congregation takes the preacher's critique seriously and will not dismiss the preacher.

Listening to Listeners Who Hear the Sermon on Ethos Settings

We can hear the above-mentioned concerns from classical rhetoric and congregational culture in the interviews from the study. Not only do many such listeners perceive the sermon as a means of relationship with the preacher, but the experience of the relationship is as important to them (perhaps more so) as the claims and recommendations of the sermon.

Traditional Ethos Concerns

The interviewees repeatedly confirm that both internal and external ethos function as described above. Many listeners do ascribe authority to the preacher because of the ministerial office and because they believe that the preacher is called by God and the church. When asked what a pastor is doing when he or she gets up to preach, one respondent says, "The thing I think they're doing is carrying out what they have been called to do. I take preaching as something that should be taken seriously, and some are called to do it; some are not called to do it." Several respondents pay attention to the sermon because the preacher is "anointed" for that task. Pastors can certainly communicate that ministry is more than "a job" in sermons, and, even more, by showing their awareness of calling in the care and reverence with which they serve each day.

Closely related is a group of listeners who take the sermon seriously because the church has designated the preacher (through training and ordination) as a representative. "A sermon has authority," says one parishioner, "because the pastor preaches it."

Listeners on ethos settings typically speak at length about the positive connection they feel with a preacher whom they see as open and caring, as we hear in the following. "Our present preacher is a very friendly, open person, very warm and very non-threatening, very non-condescending if you will. I feel like there's people you feel like you've known all your life." That feeling of long-term relationship creates a sense of trust and openness for this person. In the same vein, a long-time member of a congregation recollects an effective preacher. "The preacher was personal...would meet with you outside and talk with you there...Just a down-to-earth type person." Another listener perks up when the sermon begins because this listener sees that, outside the sanctuary, the minister "cares for *all* people and does not show favorites." Other themes are like a refrain in this body of interviews as people again and again state that they pay attention to the sermon when they sense that the pastor (in the sermon and in other life settings) is sincere, loving, caring, compassionate, down-to-earth, and has an appropriate sense of humor. One listener speaks for many, saying flatly, "The preacher's love of people gives authority to the sermon." The preacher, then, needs to relate to such listeners in ways that are down-to-earth and loving.

A fair number of people say they experience an affirming connection with the preacher when the preacher speaks in language that they can understand and in a tone that communicates the preacher's respect for the congregation.

> There are terms that are used in general church talk that the average person coming in off the street will not understand. I don't think they need to be used in the pulpit. I think that when you're in the pulpit, it needs to be down-to-earth. Bring it down. Get real.

Another listener makes a similar point when asked to cite one or two things this person would say to a roomful of preachers. "Be on the level of the people to whom you're talking. Use good English. Know your members really so well that you know to whom you're speaking and how appropriate it is."

An immediate and simple implication for preaching is obvious. The preacher should speak in language that is easily accessible to listeners.

Seeing that a minister faithfully carries out pastoral practices throughout leadership in the church assures some listeners of the quality of the preaching. An interviewee approves of the minister telling the congregation that the minister is available to talk with members any time. Another links the preacher conducting business in a business-like way with the trustworthiness of the sermon. Still another interprets the preacher visiting with members of the congregation in the pews before worship as a sign that the pastor is interested in the congregation. Thinking that the minister is interested in the people prompts this congregant to be more interested in the sermon. A number of interviewees say that the minister's regular visits in their homes raise their attentiveness to the sermon because they have the sense that the preacher has been listening to them.

Taking this concern a slightly different direction, several listeners on this setting speak with considerable passion about being put off when they sense that the preacher is speaking to them with an air of superiority. A woman wants the preacher to respect the intelligence of the congregation and concludes, succinctly, "Don't preach down to us." Another listener reports that the pastor loses credibility when the pastor seems be self-impressed and "becomes bigger than what the pastor is doing."

The preacher's dress and appearance contribute to ethos for some hearers. We can see how expectations of acceptable dress and other aspects of physical appearance vary among congregations in the following two remarks. A member of one congregation says, "One of the things I really like about the clergy in our church is that they wear vestments...I think the vestments bring that traditional presence to the pulpit." In another congregation, someone says, "As long as the preacher is clean and neat, I don't care what they wear." That appearance can affect the congregation's receptivity comes out when a long-time member of a congregation recollects a young minister who was on the staff of a large congregation and preached occasionally. "The preacher didn't wear a coat and tie when preaching for a long time. Young people don't wear coats and ties much anymore, but that bothered people." Such matters, of course, are highly contextual. One suit (or other mode of dress) does not fit all. However, preachers can at least count the dividends and costs of particular modes of dress.

While expectations of embodiment also vary a great deal, when the preacher brings the sermon to life in a way that is consistent with the mores of an individual or congregation, positive ethos usually results. We see something of the diversity in this regard in the following perceptions: one hearer prefers a pastor in the pulpit who is "a more soft-spoken, gentle person, one that can articulate well" while another prefers a preacher who is "energetic, full of life, with a booming voice and not afraid to crack the pulpit."

Integrity: A Core Value

One of the most insistent motifs in interviews of persons who listen to sermons on ethos settings is the importance of integrity between what the preacher says and how the preacher lives. While persons who hear messages on logos and pathos settings articulate the same concern, it appears with particular force among ethos-oriented listeners.

As several African American listeners say, a preacher must not only "talk the talk but walk the walk." These listeners tend to be suspicious of preachers who say one thing but live another. One person insists, "You need to be consistent between your messages and your daily life. If you're going to preach against something, and then you go out and do it, why am I going to listen to you the next day?" An older person speaks similarly. "If the preachers act one way, and they're making a sermon about something completely different, there's no integrity, and there would be no authority."

A long-term member of a congregation notices that integrity is related to broader ethos concerns.

> What goes a long way for me in a preacher is that the preacher lives the preaching. If I know him or her well enough, I know that the preaching speaks to the pastor's life. It's much more meaningful to me than if it's someone I don't know and someone that I have less respect for as a person. The life and what that life says means a lot to me. We've had a couple of women preachers here, and I've really appreciated them because their content has been nurturing, has been loving, in addition to being informative and scriptural. A personal relationship with a pastor is really what's important to me, because then I can either identify with what he or she is saying or I can affirm that his or her life is what they are saying.

Integrity and relationship creates a web within which to take preaching seriously.

A senior member of a large congregation sums up the consequences for preaching, for some listeners, when they discover that a preacher is not living with integrity. "I think you'd lose respect for the person, and if you lose respect for the person, you probably don't listen to what that person has to say."[10]

The Preacher Is Real

Another recurrent strain in listeners who approach the sermon through ethos settings is that they want to perceive the preacher as "real." They want to know the preacher has experienced the same kinds of joys and struggles they have. "We want to know that you (the preacher) are one of us." Another person says more:

> I think for me, as I think about a preacher who was particularly engaging, what impressed me or what spoke to me from [this preacher's] manner in the pulpit was this preacher's commonness. This preacher spoke like one of us, instead of like an authority. The preacher spoke as though the preacher were living it.

The interviewee comments on several positive characteristics of this pastor's sermons—the ability to leave the manuscript behind in a moment of inspiration, the use of alliteration, but the strongest point is that the preacher is "a common person."

According to these listeners, one of the important ways that preachers demonstrate that they are "one" with the congregation or "real" is through using personal experience in the pulpit. When asked to recount an engaging sermon, a listener gave a moving example of "reality" in a sermon. The past moderator and spouse of the congregation this listener attends were in their mid-thirties, and parents of two children. The spouse was dying from cancer.

> It was less of a traditional sermon. The pastor sometimes uses this methodology where they put two big chairs at the front of the church and the pastor has a dialogue with a lay person in the church. The pastor does this with...It might be a person who has been struggling with some things or has been a great example of something. I know that the pastor did one about tithing one time, but the one that recently struck me was...we had a family, and it was a gentleman who had been the past moderator of our church whose spouse was dying. The pastor was up there with the past moderator, and they had this dialogue. In essence, the past moderator gave a testimony about what faith and what our church and what the fellowship of Christians that surround him means to him, and how you deal with something as traumatic as... And the moderator's spouse subsequently passed away. You deal with having this young family and a wife who's very sick. Those things ring with you because it's very real.

This listener granted authority to the past moderator's testimony because the testimony was real: it bore the marks of actual experience with which this listener is familiar.[11]

Preachers do not have to mention profound life issues in order to communicate that they are "real," as we hear in the words of a member of another congregation:

> Maybe I get a ticket for speeding, okay? And I feel real guilty that I got a ticket. Well, the pastor has gotten a ticket for speeding and...lets you know, "Look, this happens to me." The minister lets you know that the minister sometimes has anger. The minister has to work with anger or frustration or something like that. I think the minister is terrific, but the minister has got areas, too. The preacher is just like me.

This theme is a continuous undercurrent: we identify with a preacher who is similar to us.

For the person whose settings for the sermon are in the ethos sphere, the sense that the preacher is "real" is important. This propensity suggests that preachers should make appropriate references to their own lives that are related to the content of the sermon and that prompt the perception that they are real. Ethos-oriented listeners are not distracted by the preacher's life, but, to the contrary, are actively engaged by it.

Relationship Enhances Listening

Persons who hear sermons through ethos settings report that their willingness to engage the sermon is greatly enhanced when they perceive that they have a relationship with the preacher. In smaller congregations, this perception usually results from actual day-to-day relationships with the preacher. The congregation is with the preacher in meetings at church, and in settings around town. In larger congregations, this perception often results from material in the sermon through which preachers reveal qualities of their lives with which listeners identify, especially indications that the preacher is "real."

A respondent brings this motif into relief when ruminating on one or two things this listener would like to advise preachers to improve sermons.

> Being a preacher is a very personal thing and something that I've never had my finger on it before, but when I came here it's up on one of our banners, and that is that we are personal creatures. That our personal relationships are everything. Everything we do has to do with personal relationships. Therefore, as a preacher, it's not just preaching but having the personal relationship with the people. I've been involved with preachers who are wonderful preachers, but they're not approachable. Then there's a lot lost in the relationship and in the preaching when you're not connecting.

For several listeners, a sense of personal relationship with the preacher contributes directly to the authority of the sermon.

I think having a relationship with the pastor plays a role. I think the pastor has to be open-minded. I think the pastor has to be caring. It's all right for a pastor to be smart and knowledgeable on the word of God and be able to be a good teacher and a good preacher, but the pastor must–the pastor simply must–be able to communicate and have a relationship with the people. That plays a big part in ministry, because whatever projects the pastor sets out to introduce to the people, or a vision that God gives the pastor, the people have to see something within the pastor. See that seriousness, that spirituality. I think it's important for the pastor to have a relationship with each one of the members. I think that is very important.

For this listener relationship is directly related to trustworthiness.

We hear a dramatic effect of the sense of having a relationship with a preacher from a listener who felt condemned by preachers in the past. This person now has a personal relationship with the preachers on the staff of the small church that has been this listener's congregational home for about four years.

I know where the preachers are coming from. I know that ground is level. I know this level, and I know that there's not an ounce of judgmentalism in what they're saying. I know that if they speak something, they speak it from the heart. If one of them preaches or speaks against something that I don't believe in, I will not shut it out if I know that it is something they truly believe in and that it is something they think will better me. I will never disregard it because I know that it's done in love.

Having a real relationship with these ministers allows this ethos-oriented person to consider things that, at least initially, this listener does not accept. The fact of the relationship persuades this person to be open to ideas that otherwise would be dismissed.

A member of a rural congregation in which people see one another and the pastor from day to day offers some direct suggestions for developing a relationship with the community. The interviewee recalled an earlier preacher who had "favorites" in the congregation, then suggests the following:

To me, what I think a preacher should do is have a good relationship with everybody in the congregation. Get to know them and don't have your favorites. Don't preach to one side of the room. Have the members of the congregation invite you the preacher over to their house and sit down and get to know them a little better. That way you'll have a good rapport with the people, and they'll have a good rapport with you.

Such rapport is essential for this listener. An interviewee from a very different congregational setting reinforces these ideas.

> My advice to help improve preaching would be: What's important is what happens when you're not behind the pulpit, when you're out in the congregation milling around with the congregation. I think that, to me, is the key…How much interest are you showing in your congregation? Are you checking in with people? Are you connecting? I haven't seen your wife for awhile. How is she doing? Is everything OK? Would you like me to stop by? This kind of thing. What are you needing right now? It's the human things, I think, that make a big difference in terms of how a person is perceived in the pulpit.

Note that the last line in the statement is consistent with one of the oldest emphases in ethos in rhetoric: the congregation's perception of the character of the preacher contributes directly to the congregation's willingness to attend to the sermon. Caring for people outside the sermon enhances the congregation's receptivity to the preacher.

The following citation speaks for a fair number of persons who process the sermon through ethos settings but do not perceive the preacher as a person who is concerned with relationships.

> Never really got to be as close with [that preacher as with another one with whom the interviewee felt quite close and whom the interviewee regarded as a strong preacher]. I think [the preacher from whom the listener felt distant] had a hard time fitting in with the community. I think it was something the minister was not prepared for. The minister thought it was going to be something other than what it was in reality. It didn't seem as if the call of that preacher to this congregation was a good fit. The locale and the type of person the preacher was, not that the minister came in and made enemies or anything like that. The minister just never really developed that closeness. It was always kind of a standoffish situation where that person was the pastor of the church, but was more an administrator rather than what I think of as a pastor, or a shepherd of a flock relationship. It was more like a CEO in an organization.

As a consequence, this person remained distant not only from the preacher as person but also from sermons.

In a comment that lays a bridge to the next section, another person points out that while a relationship with a preacher involving time together in the same space and time is ideal, the sense of relationship is really key even when a lot of personal time is not involved.

Our minister is a friend. The minister has become a friend, but has become almost a parental figure. The minister is the teacher and I'm the student. This minister has taught me a lot. The minister is very hard-working, so you have to respect that, because the minister backs up words with actions. The minister is very nice...and very loving...and really accessible and human and honest and nice. I see the minister pretty much just on Sundays. We were part of the same Bible study series last time. So it kinda feels like the minister is part of my family, but it's not like I talk to the minister every day or anything like that.

Although the interviewee does not in fact see the preacher a lot face to face, the interviewee has the sense of being in relationship with the preacher.

For a handful of people, relationship supercedes all other concerns. After expressing sorrow that many people who had been members of the church for many years have been moving into a residence for senior citizens sponsored by the denomination but too far for them to return for worship, the listener says, poignantly, "For me it is a lot about relationships." Wanting to know the referent of "it" in the preceding sentence, the interviewer asks, "The preaching?" to which the respondent clarifies:

"All the people. Not the preaching. The people. So if there were no message, it would be still we're worshipping as a group and you would still feel the need that you would want to get together with those people. Say our ministers didn't even show up. We're going to have service. We're still going to come and worship. There's just not going to be what we had. I still think those people would want to get together. I've seen other folks—maybe they'll get mad about something and go away. I don't see how they can do that."

The fact of being together is, in essence, the message for this listener.

An important implication for preaching is that the minister needs to demonstrate active, caring, loving relationships with the congregation. We noted above that many parishioners take pastoral calling in the home, office, and school as a sign of care. While some pastors claim they "do not have time to call," parishioners in some congregational cultures find that calling (and other means of getting to know people) contributes directly to these listeners' willingness to entertain the sermon.

Sermon as Perception of Relationship

Some listeners perceive the sermon itself as an experience of relationship with the pastor. A member of a large congregation has just said that a feeling of relationship with the pastor is important. "In terms of preaching, I think that's the way many people relate with their pastors. If you don't have a going out for coffee relationship with your pastor, many times that sermon is the way they speak to you. Even though you're in a crowd, they're speaking to you individually."

Still another person who has attended worship regularly for many years says, "I have trouble remembering sermons in content. I relate preaching more to the pastor and his or her life than I do to the content." The listener explains why:

> That's wrapped up with personal identity and personal relationships. I don't think sermons are separate from that. It isn't just content. It's life. It's the whole life. When I know a pastor is speaking from his or her life, her own experience and their values and the way they live their life, the sermon is much more meaningful. I don't care what they're saying.

The interview as a whole makes it clear that the sermon is an experience of relationship within which the listener encounters some content.

Setting the stage for a similar point, another respondent contrasts some preachers "who were like members of the family" with "others who I felt were just talking to me. There were some preachers…I attended for years, and never felt they knew my name. I've always said that the saddest thing I've ever seen is a funeral preached by a preacher who didn't know the name of the deceased." Indeed, of some people in the ministry, this listener remarks, "I just felt like it was a job. Come in Sunday morning, read a sermon off the page, shake a few hands and go home." The listener comments that a close relationship with the pastor does result in a closer connection in preaching.

> I don't know if it's a cause and effect relationship. In other words, I don't know if I felt that the sermons were more personal because of my relationship, or they were more personal just because they were more personal people. But somehow I felt more in tune with those people. It may be that I was hearing their voice, the same voice that I heard in other settings. It might be that I could see the examples that they lived out in their lives. Certainly, I felt closer to those people, and therefore, more in touch with their messages.

A feeling of positive relationship with the preacher is a significant part of the message.

Occasional listeners speak of being with the congregation while hearing the sermon as having theological import.

> I think that the message, from the two ministers in the congregation, tend to serve as a connector point for a lot of people. In other words, we all sort of come together and we know as we sit and listen to this message that we're all a part of a bigger picture. I know I've been uplifted at times, and I know I've felt sad, and I

know I've felt emotional, but I think it's nice to turn and to look at other people and to realize that we're all in here listening to this message at the same time, and that carries through the rest of the week.

Preaching is a moment in which this listener feels connected not only with the preacher but also with the rest of the congregation.

Another listener provides a philosophical and theological rationale for regarding relationship at the center of preaching. Reflecting on the failure of the sermon of a visiting preacher to intersect with the congregation, a listener says that the sermon's troubles began at the beginning when the preacher started the sermon in a way that was disconnected from the life of the congregation. "When preachers just launch right in, I feel like 'Who are you?' When if it seems like they're making some assumptions about the congregation that I feel are unfair, at that point I've already decided they don't know us, so why should I listen?" The interviewee expands:

> The visiting minister said something about, "I think a lot of the time we come to church and want it to be a spa instead of a workout. So we come, and we want to feel better." I thought, "Do you know who these people are that you're saying this to? The people at this church work really hard. Many people are here more than once during the week packing up bag lunches or delivering food to the needy. There's this entire Bible study where we have some serious issues that they're struggling with. I just don't get a spa mentality from this congregation at all." This is just an example of feeling like he didn't do his research on who he was talking to.

The interviewer responds, "If you don't have a relationship with them, then it's harder to listen." "Right," continues the interviewee, "*But everyone has a relationship with everyone else.* So it's not hard to remind people of what that is" (my emphasis). For this relationship is the structure of reality.

Ethos Settings Interact with Logos

The person who takes in the sermon through ethos settings is also affected by logos and pathos settings and shares important things with these other listeners. Most of the people interviewed, for instance, identify teaching as a primary purpose of the sermon. They also say that they like sermons that are well organized and that draw out the implications of the sermon for their everyday worlds. Persons who process sermons on ethos wavelengths, however, voice logos emphases that are distinctive of ethos orientations. While these themes appear occasionally in interviews from the logos and pathos cohorts, they recur repeatedly in interviews with an ethos base.

The distinctive logos themes in folk who hear the sermon with ethos accents mainly have to do with what the preacher says about relationship with God, with others, and service in the community. While many of these listeners respond positively to material in the sermon that arises from the preacher's own life, I do not find that these listeners prefer particular forms or styles of preaching.

Relationship with God

Most of the hearers on ethos settings directly mention that they seek guidance in relationship with God from sermons. One of the most articulate listeners says, plainly:

> I think that what ultimately a good sermon does is it makes you think about your relationship with God and how you live your life and how you might live your life differently in order to get closer to God and the spiritual and relational paths. A good sermon will make you think about those things. It might not get you there today, but it will make you think about them.

The following listener expresses a view of God that explains how some persons who listen through ethos settings understand God in relationship to relationships (so to speak).

> I have a very expansive view of God. I sort of think God is everywhere, in every human being, in my children. So I don't think that it's that different in church. It's just that it's a time to be quiet and engage in your thoughts and feelings and behaviors at least once a week if you can't do it any other time, and that reminds you as you set about your new week how to be more inclusive and to think more about those issues. For me, it's not God is here and God is nowhere else or that kind of thing. It's much more about taking some time out in a busy life to really think about what matters and to feel more connected to God than you might in a normal day, although there are lots of other times when I do.

For this person, one purpose of the sermon is to bring into focus the relationship with God that is omnipresent. The preacher can help this listener consider how the listener's relationship with God affects all other relationships, and (insofar as possible) should help this listener become cognizant of (and responsive to) the divine presence at all times.

Another member of the study group responds to the question, "What do you most want to know about God when you hear a sermon?" by showing how the interest in learning about relationship with God intersects with other values that are important to folk on ethos settings. "I want to know about how God would want me to live my life today. How I should walk with God and how I should live as a Christian, and just how I should be living a Christian life and relating to other people."

Many other persons who sit in the pews with ethos ears share this intermingled concern: they want the sermon to teach them about relating with God and about how their relationship with God affects other relationships.

> I believe the sermon should have something in it that points us to God. I believe the sermon should have nurturing and affirmation and affirm God's grace and love. Usually that happens regardless of what age the person is. On Sunday morning, we need to be called to account for our membership, for our baptismal vow, whatever vows we took in terms of membership, and our discipleship.

For this member, the Christian life has a definite communal character: she wants the preacher to help her realize how awareness of God's love should call her to take responsibility for living in baptismal covenant with others.

From the point of view of the following listener, the sermon that helps the congregation accept God's love for them, and for all, has significant social consequences.

> I just know God loves me. I just feel that love covers everything. I feel that if you love, if you truly love, these things that we're not supposed to do, we won't do. If I love you, I'm not going to steal from you. I'm not going to lie to you. I'm not going to kill you. All these things should be tempered by love. Some people who don't like a person and they won't speak to them. Well, they need to get together. If I had somebody I didn't like, I'm going to go to you and we're going to get it on. We might have to fight, but we will get through with the love.

Many of these listeners want the preacher to help them know more about relating with God, because that will help them relate better to other people.

A sermon that helps these folk explore their relationship with God will seem helpful to these listeners. Furthermore, the preacher can help these listeners become even more interested by including material in the sermon that encourages them to consider how their relationship with God impacts their relationships with other people.

Relationship with Other People

Another common desire in congregants who follow the sermon on ethos settings is for sermons to encourage relationship with one another and to promote a sense of community within the congregation. An interviewer asked, "What do you think the pastor is doing when he or she stands up to preach?" To this question a respondent sounded a bell that reverberates through the interviews with others. "I think a lot of times that depends on the person who's standing up to speak and what their views are theologically, but I think that ideally the preacher is standing up to call together the people of God and to continue to form the community of God and to join people together as one in that act." The listeners on the ethos band recurrently talk about preaching "unifying the congregation," "bringing people together," and "building up the body."

When asked how preaching shapes the congregation, a person introduces two long examples to show the importance of preaching in developing community even when a congregation is conflicted.

> I think there are times when there are issues confronting the church. At our previous congregation, we rearranged the whole worship space and made it more open and pulled the pulpit down and made it much more accessible to the people. There was a lot of talk across different sermons about what we're trying to accomplish with our physical space, which then is consistent with these kinds of themes that are in our religious teachings. I think that was very useful. It was very helpful for people. I thought it was a great idea regardless of hearing it in the sermon, but I think it really kind of helped bring people together and helped them think differently about space. So that's one example of where I think preaching shaping a congregation happened. I remember a couple of sermons about stewardship that I thought were particularly good and that helped people think about stewardship differently. I was one of the team leaders of stewardship one year, and it was helpful for me to hear stewardship thought of as less about just giving money and trying to get people to pledge, but more about what it would do for the church and what the church would be able to do as group if we were able to have people really support the church financially.

For this listener, as for many others who listen on ethos settings, preaching on relationship helps the congregation maintain a vital sense of life and mission.

Several folk who tune into preaching through ethos settings mention that sermons have prompted them to repair broken relationships.

> It seems to me that I had to listen to a sermon on forgiveness at a time when I was really, really angry with someone. I don't remember very well the specifics, but it seems to me that I was going through the whole thing, looking for little mini logical points to argue so that I didn't have to agree with the whole premise. I think in the end that I had to go home and think about it a little more before I mended my ways.

Despite the discomfort that the sermon caused this listener, the person did, indeed, act on the sermon's premise to restore relationship by seeking forgiveness.

Despite the desire for the sermon to unify the congregation, several of the individuals who hear the sermon from ethos points of view recognize plurality within the congregation. When asked what preaching does, for instance, one person replies:

> I think it gives one unified message from the leader, the spiritual shepherd, of this congregation. All ears hear the same thing. I'm sure all ears pick out different points and hang onto other things and discard those that they don't want to hear. We're all like that, especially when you're challenged in an area, where you're uncomfortable. I think it's easy to hang onto the topics or at least parts of the sermon that don't challenge you as much as others.

This listener encourages preachers to include material in the sermon that stretches hearers. "I do enjoy coming every Sunday to receive some sort of challenge to make me think about things I wouldn't have thought of possibly on my own, or to highlight things from the Bible that on my own I may not be pushed to think about very hard or very long." Others, this listener thinks, need the same kind of push.

The preacher who wants to develop logos with these listeners in mind can talk about how the gospel helps the listeners enrich their relationships with one another. Sermons can name barriers to relationships and show how the listeners can become a community.

Reach Out to the World Beyond the Congregation

The theme of wanting the sermon to point them to service beyond the congregation runs through many interviews with people on ethos settings. This concern is a natural outgrowth of the turn toward relationality that permeates this setting. This point is one of the few in the transcripts at which I see more emphasis in one racial and ethnic community than in the other. African Americans articulate more strongly the desire for the sermon to guide them in service outside the congregation than persons of non-Hispanic European origin.

The desire for the sermon to point the way to service in the community is at the core of this African American listener's comments about the preacher and preaching:

> A minister for me has to be somebody that I can feel good about, that I can relate to, that treats everyone equally. I want the preacher to energize me, to show me a way to help. I believe in helping. For that minister to give me a sermon that will show me how I can help or do things that would be an energizer where I can say, "Oh, yes. That would be something I can do."

This listener thinks service is part of the congregation's identity as evidenced in ways in which the congregation is involved in the community, e.g., by sponsoring dinners at the end of the month for households who run out of money. One reason the dinners succeed is that sermons encourage people to support them.

Another listener attests that the most important things that happen in the life of the congregation are acts of service that the congregation performs in the wider community. This respondent spends several hours delivering meals each week. The congregant explains how the sermon and the preacher foster the congregation's attitude to serve.

> I guess [our denomination] has a reputation of being involved in the community. I've seen what we've done over the years to get involved. You have people that do get filled with the Spirit and they respond. When I was younger I wasn't involved in it as much because I was like, "Hey, anybody can do that." That's true. Everybody can do it, but people need to be involved... I think from the sermons and Bible studies, that's where you're seeing the involvement. And the preacher has to say, "Hey, we have a grand vision."

The interviewer adds a comment heard in another context in the congregation to the effect that the pastor is "living out some of that involvement in front of the congregation." "Yes," the interviewee notes, "I think because the pastor is always here. The pastor is involved in the community. In a lot of things. It sort of rubs off on you."

When asked how preaching shapes the congregation as a community, a person says, "I think it provides a clear example of what is important and where this church is going," and follows with an example of the congregation supporting a project to provide animals that people in other countries can raise for food. The interviewer asks, "How does preaching come together with the church doing that project?"

> We were challenged, I think, as a congregation to extend ourselves beyond our community and the people we see everyday to people we may never see, to situations we may never know, and to try to become sympathetic to them and available to help in a way we can. Maybe we can't go over there and help build a school or clothe a person directly, but what we can do is from our little place here in [our state] offer avenues for that–the [animal] project, the [walk for hunger], and things like that. So the challenge is laid out first and then possible ways to accept the challenge.

Service to others arises in part because the congregant feels a relationship with the situation of others. Here, of course, we are reminded of the interweaving of themes in listeners as we also see pathos ("sympathetic to") influencing this listener's response to the preacher's appeal to become involved.

A sermon (or a part of a sermon) that points to opportunities for expressing relationship with the broader world via service outside the congregation will appeal to these folk. The last respondent, above, points to an important part of such discussion by intimating that the preacher could indicate "possible ways to accept the challenge," that is, practical guidance to help the listener engage in actual acts of service.

Personal Experience of the Preacher

While folk who receive the sermon by way of ethos settings do not specify particular forms of preaching to which they are drawn, they indicate that they respond well when preachers use personal experience. A hearer points to one of the important pastoral effects of such material. "In every one of the sermons the pastor can pull a life experience into it and relate it to you as a human being. 'I know someone who went through this.'" Knowing that other people have made it through difficult experiences encourages this hearer to believe that the hearer, too, can make it through.

When asked to recall a sermon that was a high point, one interviewee points to the interrelationship of self-disclosure, struggle, and memorability.

> I think that the things I remember are often when a minister or someone preaching will personalize the sermon a little bit. Disclose a little bit of something about him or herself that shows that person has grappled with the issues. That person is only human after all, as we all are. That person doesn't put himself or herself above the congregation in some way. I think those things, when they're connected to the main theme, or less, for me, are really poignant, and oftentimes those are things that I remember long after a lot of the other material.

These listeners place a premium on knowing the preacher's own struggles with regard to the issues of the sermon:

> I particularly am drawn into the sermons that deal with the struggle for personal faith. An example would be the sermon a member of the congregation gave when pastor was out and that person was a guest in the pulpit. That sermon was connecting with me because I think that struggle is something that everybody struggles with at one point or maybe at many points in their faith growth journey. To listen to another person openly and honestly witness to their own faith helps at times to connect and help me over a struggling point that I may have that they may have already gone through, and now can help me go through.

Another listener echoes the same theme:

> I really love the sermons that are about things that we're uncomfortable about and the times when ministers say, "You know, I just don't get this. I just really don't understand this, but here's what I've been thinking about." I love it when people get up and say, "I'm struggling with you on this."

This interviewee encourages the preacher actually to wrestle with issues (even unresolved ones) in the pulpit. The awareness that the preacher is doing so creates a real sense of relationship with this listener.

Resonating similarly, another member of a study congregation recollects what was engaging about a sermon in which the preacher made some self-confession.

> The preacher's honesty. The preacher's brokenness. So many times as humans and especially as preachers, as people who are expected to be looked up to and be perfect. You know what I mean. We're afraid to be honest and vulnerable because somebody else is paying our paycheck, or because we're afraid of being spiritually judged. I guess that goes back to the biblical David who was pretty out there. David messed up. David would go down on the face. David could have tried to hide what David had done or argue with Nathan...but David didn't. And like the preacher, we share that with each other. There are going to be those few that are going to go, "Huh," and they'll get their little spiritual tails up in a roar, but for the majority, to me it's a witness as to how we're all supposed to be. Because Jesus was vulnerable and Jesus was all those things even though Jesus was perfect, but the point was Jesus gave Jesus' self to those disciples, and Jesus was who Jesus was. I think that's why the sermon was so engaging.

This listener is not only engaged by the preacher's honesty and admission of brokenness but finds a relational connection with David, Jesus, and the listener's own life.

The preacher can attract many people who hear the sermon on ethos wavelengths into the world of the sermon by speaking about the preacher's own life and experience. Of course, the material included in the sermon needs to be appropriate for public discussion and needs to relate to the major concerns of the sermon.

Ethos Settings Interact with Pathos

As noted previously the person who takes in the sermon through ethos settings is affected by pathos, but they voice pathos emphases that relate to overarching ethos concerns. Feeling is typically important to people on ethos settings as it deepens the listener's perception of relationship with the preacher, the congregation, or God.

The following report illustrates how pathos helps create a sense of relationship for many persons who listen to the sermon through ethos settings. Here we see that for some folk who listen to the sermon on ethos settings, the sense of relationship with others often involves a significant degree of feeling. When asked to give a positive example of being stirred emotionally, the listener recalls:

I'm here. It's my first Christmas away from my family. I'm by myself. It [my circumstance] did stir emotions, but it stirred the emotion of I was lonely. I was scared. I had just moved 900 miles from home. I was twenty-two years old. I took on a job working with a big corporation. I had a lot of responsibility on me. I had just walked out of school. I had been in college for three years, but I had my first break in corporate America, and I was not going to let that go. I had a lot of uncertainties. Then again, the preacher that night, the emotion that the preacher put into telling the stories of the Christmas Eve services with the minister's parents, that emotion, the emotion of love that the preacher gave out is what made the sermon.

The listener meditates, "That was the first time I came here, and I knew I was home." The listener identified with the preacher by experiencing love through the sermon.

"You can have all of the knowledge of scripture in the world, but if you do not have a genuine love for people and a compassion for people, none of it really matters because you'll talk over their heads. They've got to feel it here [interviewee touches heart] not here [interviewee touches head]. To the person, the ear is not as sensitive as the heart is. I think the preacher is pretty much down-to-earth, and keeps with the times. I think the preacher understands what people go through. The preacher knows where this twenty-five year old has been.

This listener continues to experience a relationship of love with this preacher and to find that the congregation is, indeed, a long-term "home," that is, a community in which the listener experiences "unconditional love."

The interaction between ethos and pathos often has an even more communal dimension as we hear expressed by a listener who thinks about what happens when an African American congregation is stirred as a sermon reaches its climax.[12]

Well, I think it's good because people are giving praise to God. You feel connected to other people when you see they have a similar response to the sermon. So I think that's one of the good things. You realize when you hear a sermon, hey, you're not out there by yourself. This faith walk we have, we're all on common ground, so we're all trying to be perfected in Christ. We're being molded and shaped each day. So we see other people kind of reacting to the sermon in the same way that you are, and that shows that you're connected to other people.

A number of other listeners comment similarly. The awareness of shared emotion is for them an experience of connection or relationship with other people.

Pathos generated through the sermon can power ethos-oriented listeners to act in Christian witness.

> I know that in our former congregation there was a visiting preacher who was in the trenches in Africa and talked a great deal about HIV and the problems there. I was very moved by that. I also remember another sermon by a person there, who wasn't a minister, who was working and visiting with prisoners regularly and talked about those experiences and how God fit into all of that. I remember being really moved by this person's commitments to that as well as thinking differently about prisoners and their needs. These are two that I remember off the top of my head.

The interviewer comments, "It's the personal story," which prompts further response:

> I know that the preachers did their work in connecting it with the readings that day, but I remember the stories more. Yes. And they set examples for me as I think about how I lead my life when I hear people who spend all of their time helping others. It's just an amazing...I'm so in awe of that. And the challenges. I think both of those individuals were doing a lot of that. Touched me.

The interviewer asks if there was a congregation-wide emotional response to the sermon.

> I think the one about Africa and HIV was pretty...I remember the collection of money to send with this fellow went off the deep end. People were pretty touched by it. That one I think in particular really reached out to folks, and people really felt connected and felt like a community.

The ethos setting functions for this listener as a kind of lens through which pathos flows. The listener is "touched," but in a way that facilitates relationship. The experience of pathos is not only an internal feeling for this listener but a source of power for expressing relationship with others.

In the following comment, a listener rues what this person perceives as emotional abuse by preachers.

> Emotions, I feel, in the church when in the context of sermons, are sometimes abused. I think that sometimes minister will use emotions. They use emotions as a button to push people to make them accept one particular idea or to actually turn them off of something else. Sometimes I know of ministers that would stretch the truth blatantly. I caught a minister at that. Down home at this point when I was in college I was traveling to other churches and things. I was with that minister when the particular instance happened. That minister turned the whole story completely around

and pried on that congregation's emotions to push a point, but it was not true. It was a lie.

The detrimental effect of the emotional abuse perpetrated by the preacher was compounded by the fact that the listener knew that the preacher had violated one of the fundamental requirements for positive ethos: the preacher lied.

Some listeners who receive the sermon through ethos channels say they do not respond positively to emotion in the preacher or in the congregation. Some simply say, "I am not an emotional person." This is true of some members of the African American community such as the following listener who is a member of a church that worships in a high liturgical style.

> I'm not a real emotional person, and ours is not a church that encourages emotionalism. That's one of the reasons why we joined this church, because it's not. You don't have exhibitionists here. This is not to criticize or degrade people who like to shout. That's all right for them if it's what they feel they want to do, but the [name of denomination] Church is not that kind of a church.

The preacher, then, cannot assume that listeners will inherently perceive the presence of pathos as positive (or negative). The preacher needs to learn how pathos functions in the congregational culture, and how particular listeners respond to it.

One of my friends, hearing me describe persons who listen to the sermon on ethos settings declared, "Those people are so mesmerized by relationship that they would have a spiritual experience if the preacher stood and read the phone book just because it is the preacher." This statement is vastly overdrawn, of course, but it does point to an essential characteristic of many people who receive the sermon through ethos. Their perception of the preacher (and their sense of relationship with the preacher and with the congregation) is a significant dimension of the experience of hearing a sermon.

While the qualities that we have identified in this chapter are distinctive of listening on ethos settings, these qualities are not unique to such persons. Indeed, the qualities associated with ethos vary in strength from one person on this setting to another. As we will see in the next two chapters, persons who listen to the sermon through logos and pathos settings manifest characteristics typically (but not uniquely) associated with ethos. Nevertheless, a preacher can profitably ask of every sermon, "What kinds of material do I need to include to help engage listeners who hear the sermon through ethos settings?"

CHAPTER 3

Logos Settings

In the early pages of this book, we recounted a brief vignette about Lorenzo, a long- time member of a congregation, who came to the pastor after the morning service with the appreciative response, "I am really interested in the big idea you developed in the sermon. Could you give me the title of a book that develops that idea more fully?" While the sermon contained vivid language, an easy-to-follow structure, some tension and drama, emotionally moving illustrations drawn from real life, and was embodied in a warm and engaging way in the pulpit, this listener was arrested by the idea itself. For Lorenzo, encountering a significant idea is essential to a satisfying experience of hearing a sermon. When a sermon does not contain an idea that Lorenzo perceives as important, this listener leaves the sermon disappointed or frustrated.

Many other people have an orientation to the sermon that is similar to Lorenzo's. The interviews that led to this book reveal that many persons listen to the sermon through logos settings. They are most concerned with the thoughts that preachers develop in sermons. These listeners tend to experience other aspects of the sermon—ethos, pathos, and embodiment—through logos.

In this chapter, I first recap the traditional picture of logos in rhetoric. The heart of the chapter focuses on the words of interviewees who receive the sermon through logos settings to allow them to describe how logos functions for them. We then turn to ways that listeners on logos settings interact with pathos and ethos material. Along the way, I call attention to things a preacher can do to increase the likelihood that people on logos settings will respond positively to the appeal of the sermon.

Characteristics of Logos in Rhetoric

In classical rhetoric, logos refers to how the speaker appeals to the audience by developing the content of the speech. Different approaches to development have different strengths and weaknesses, and suit different occasions.[1] Logos includes the reasons (warrants) and other types of reasoning and evidence that a speaker uses inside a speech to urge the audience to accept the claims the speaker presents. It includes, further, appeals to ideas and themes that are recognized by the audience or that the speaker thinks will be persuasive to the listeners. Logos dimensions of the sermon include appeals to patterns of logic such as inductive or deductive, as well as genres of the speech that both serve the purposes of the speech and that the audience admires. An accomplished communicator often cites authorities whose opinions the listeners respect (and whose opinions are likely to be convincing to the listeners). A preacher, for instance, will appeal to the Bible, and perhaps to tradition, experience, and reason. Such communicators also bring into the address ideas, practices, and values that those hearing the address assume to be true; hopefully, they will project that sense of truthfulness onto the rhetor's address.

Lucy Lind Hogan and Robert Stephen Reid, leading authorities on the significance of rhetoric for preaching, summarize when they say, "Logos, in rhetoric, is concerned with actively thinking about and reflecting on the situation, and then making appropriate choices of words and arguments, given the situation, the listeners, and God's call to bold proclamation."[2] The preacher, like other speakers, aims to present the congregation with persuasive reasons for adopting the ideas or actions commended in the sermon. Indeed, per our comments on congregational culture earlier, one of the speaker's primary responsibilities is to determine to what kinds of reasoning and genres of communication the congregation is likely to respond positively.

Although logos, in traditional rhetoric focuses primarily upon the arguments that a speaker relies upon to convince listeners to adopt a point of view, the interviewees in our study think about logos concerns to include not only patterns of logic and argument, but more broadly of aspects of preaching that help them interpret the meaning of life. Logos includes not only formal logic and other modes of data that help a congregation consider the validity of an idea, but also examples, illustrations, and even images that bring the key claims of the sermon to expression.[3] Theoreticians in the field of preaching notice, further, that some homilies function as experiences of the imagination. From this latter point of view, the hearer is persuaded less by responding to arguments and more as a result of entering the imaginative world of the sermon much like a reader enters the world of a novel or movie. The import of the message comes to the listeners via participation in the imaginative experience of the sermon.[4]

Like ethos, logos is also highly contextual. A thoughtful pastor will consider how to shape the sermon so that it can have an optimum appeal to a particular congregation. The preacher will employ forms of reasoning or experience that are at home in the congregation, or that the congregation can quickly recognize. As we see in the following interviews, individuals and congregations place different values on different forms of argument and content. The pastor needs to listen carefully to the congregation to determine what kinds of material the members find more (and less) convincing.

Listening to Listeners Who Hear the Sermon on Logos Settings

The listeners in our study who hear the sermon on logos channels seem less concerned about particular forms or genres whereby the content of the sermon is developed, and more interested in the fact of significant content clearly expressed. Like Lorenzo, they want the sermon to help them interpret the meaning of life in conceptual terms. Traditional logos concerns are important for many of these hearers in connection with clarity, consistency, and credibility. Many of them want the sermon to be clear. For a lot of these listeners, in fact, the sermon must have at least one discernible point. They want the logic of the sermon to be internally consistent, and to be consistent with other things that the church believes and does. They also want the sermon to be intellectually credible. In other words, they want to be able to believe that the major points of the sermon are true. In the materials that follow, interviewees expand on these themes and refract them through their individual and congregational contexts.

What Would Be Missing If There Were No Sermon?

As I have commented previously, most of the themes associated with one setting also appear (though with less frequency and intensity) in connection with other settings. Concern for integrity, for instance, while distinctive of persons who listen on ethos settings is also found in listeners from logos and pathos settings. One theme, however, is found almost exclusively in one setting. To the alarm of authorities in the field of worship, half a dozen persons in our study who hear the sermon through logos settings say that they themselves would be missing from worship if there were no sermon. While this response is not shared (at least in this bald form) by others who follow the sermon from logos perspectives, when we join these remarks with many others concerning the purpose of preaching, we realize that this remark hints at a primary reason that many of the members of this cohort come to church: They want the sermon to help them discover the meaning of life so that they can respond appropriately.[5]

When asked, "What would be missing if there were no sermon?" a listener responds, "Probably me." Another says, "Half the service at least. If there were no sermon, what would be the point of coming?" A member of a denomination in which the sermon is typically followed by a period of congregational sharing thinks of these two events as "the two masts of this whole congregation." In a congregation that partakes of the breaking of the loaf every Sunday, a life-long attendee still speaks of the sermon as "the heart and soul of worship." Another person in the same tradition, who testifies to the importance of the sacred meal, agrees that if the sermon were missing, "It would be worse than worship without communion."[6]

Several listeners comment on how the service "leads up to the sermon." One colorful interviewee says:

> I always refer to the sermon as the main event. In other words, I think everything else leads up to that. It's kind of like going to dinner, and you don't get the main course. You may have some desserts, and you may have some appetizers, which are always nice, but if you don't get the main course, then you missed something.

Similarly, someone else in the study says, "The word is the important thing. All the service is built around the sermon. The music is tied into it. The liturgy is tied into the sermon. Everything is tied into the sermon."[7]

Wanting Information and Ideas

People involved in the sermon through logos settings reveal much of what they seek in a sermon when they discuss the purposes of preaching. These hearers almost universally agree that a major purpose of preaching is to communicate information and ideas that help them interpret the significance of the Bible and the gospel for life. These listeners seek encounter with ideas (especially about God and the meaning of life) they have not previously engaged. "Give me the one thing I demand out of sermons. It would be content."

These concerns come out in the following comments that come from interviewees who are male and female, African American and persons of non-Hispanic European origin, and congregations of various sizes, denominations, and locations.

When asked what preaching does that other things in the congregation do not do, a listener says:

> The sermon is the time, particularly for people who aren't going to Sunday school, to make sure we keep learning different things from the Bible and keep connecting our faith with the real world. That's not something you can get necessarily by yourself. The sermon is a chance to actually get that information from someone who is educated in the field and can help bring to light some thing you may not think about and that you won't get just in the rest of your conversations with people, even within the church... Educational, yes, that's probably the biggest thing I would see.

The fact that the preacher is educated is an ethos element, but it serves a logos concern: the preacher's education is important because it is the source of information.

A number of folk, especially from congregations in the long-established denominations in which Sunday school attendance is declining, look to the sermon as a primary event of teaching and learning. "Only a limited number of people come to Sunday school, so the sermon is an opportunity for there to be some teaching about the Christian life and the Bible and also maybe provide some material for thought relative to the Christian life during the week."

The perception that the sermon is an event of learning is a kind of central nervous system in many interviews of persons who hear the sermon on logos settings. I take one as representative. "Preaching," says one such person, "keeps me coming back because I am learning as I go. I like applying the scripture to whatever they're talking about. That helps me." In contrast, in a previous church, "we weren't taught anything" by the sermons. Learning more, for this person, should be the primary result of a sermon. "I want to come away with something I've been taught that I need to make myself better, help my family better, something to teach myself." Preaching has a synthesizing function. "You need that preaching to tie what a person learns in Sunday school, Bible study, devotional books, etc. all in together and to teach you how to live it daily." If there were no sermon, "Gosh, then, how would they learn? Some people don't do any other studying, any other praying, other than listening to the preacher. That's why the preacher needs to be good."

Many who take in the sermon on logos settings are engaged by sermons that prompt them to think about new ideas, or to think afresh about familiar ones. As one says, "Just in general terms the sermon lets you think about something you never thought about before or think about it in a different way." Another hearer articulates the same preference and offers an illustration.

> For me, it should open up an issue in a new way and give me insight. If it takes that passage in Job…and allows me to look at it in a new light and gives me additional information about. I'm seeking, I'm looking to know God. When the sermon is about something where God is revealed to me, that is what really makes a good sermon for me. That sermon on Job was important because it made me look at things differently. It made me think about things differently. There's insight there. If they get up and the sermon is just on something they've preached on fifty times before, and they don't have anything new to say about it, that's not nearly as meaningful as taking a scripture apart and explaining to me what it might mean.

In other remarks, this listener acknowledges that the preacher is not simply a source of "information" but is actually offering an interpretation of some aspect of God's relationship with the world.

Quite a few listeners are grateful when the sermon prompts them to think in a fresh way, even when they do not agree with the preacher. An interviewee remembers of a preacher in the past, "The sermons were very good, very thought-provoking. You didn't always agree with that preacher, but at least the sermons made you think. I like that." Another listener is asked whether a sermon can have authority when it articulates something with which the listener does not immediately agree.

> If it's presented in a way that is intellectually stimulating and causes me to think about the issue, at least question, sure. I don't think I'm right all the time. I think this whole business of traveling through religion from childhood to adulthood is a constant learning experience. You're always changing and coming up with different ideas, hopefully gaining insight. I think you are always learning until you reach a point where you can't do it anymore.

For this listener, as for many others, "My mind has been evolving over a period of time, having different perspectives from different people and different cultures." This listener says of preachers, "I listen to what they say and try to internalize it as best I can, and come up with my understanding of what they're trying to say."

Some listeners, such as the one who made this remark, actively look for sermons to push their thinking. "The preacher challenges your ways of thinking about the scripture that the preacher is addressing at the time. I call it my old way of saying about it. The preacher challenges that and causes you to think."

Congregants attuned to the message on logos settings are particularly interested in theological issues. Many of them leave no doubt as to what they most want to learn about. "I think that I have so much that I need to know about God." Indeed, this question is a central point of connection for members of a congregation whose membership is quite diverse. "Age, race, income levels, educational levels. I think everybody comes here for the primary purpose of learning more about God, Jesus, and the Bible." Many of the persons in the interview group are aware of the fact that all human knowledge about God is necessarily limited. However, such questions are existentially important, as we hear in another listener's example:

> I know that there is little to know about God other than what we can find in the Bible and what God reveals to us in our hearts. Of course, there are many questions I can't wait to ask when I get to heaven. Like, for example, "Why do we suffer?" I think I kind of know basically that it's just a part of the world, and we live in the

world. How can we be immune from the world and the laws of this world? How can we exist in the world and be immune from the world? So that is why we suffer like everyone else. It rains on the good and the evil.

The interviewer asks if the interviewee looks for the sermon to answer such questions.

Yes. Often. Often I do. Like, "How will our pastor answer this question that I've wondered about for so long? What approach will the pastor take?" Usually I find that the pastor takes similar types of questions that are important to me and the pastor usually has similar answers, but I often find that the pastor has found something slightly different or that the pastor has something to add to it. I really appreciate that. Like the pastor has thought a little bit deeper or taken a little bit different approach to it and has found a little bit of a different answer. I appreciate that.

Many logos hearers acknowledge that while they know that they cannot have complete knowledge of God and God's ways, they want to know as much as they can.

Quite a few persons who listen to sermons on logos settings speak forcefully about the importance of the preacher offering a rationale for the major claims in the sermon. "I like it," says one, "when the preachers talk about how to behave, how to conduct your life, what to do. Then not just *what* to do but *why* you should do it that way, and where the foundation, and where the authority for that is." Another listener goes further in interpreting an excellent quality in the preaching of the senior minister.

The senior minister explains. The senior minister doesn't just come out, "This is wrong because I say it's wrong." This minister looks for scriptural backing and reminds us, "What do you think Jesus Christ would say about this if Jesus were here today? What would Jesus' stand be?" The senior minister is effective in giving reasons for the stands this minister takes. The senior minister doesn't just say, "Believe this because I am your pastor and I tell you this is what you ought to believe." The minister will say, "This is why. This is my stand on this issue." The senior minister gives a logical defense or apologetics of why that's the stand.

Pressing ahead, this listener explains why it is important for the preacher to provide a rationale for beliefs and other matters pertaining to Christian life.

I'm concerned that people don't know a lot of times what they believe and if they've got a belief their statement is, "What do you believe?" "Well, I believe what the church believes." "Well, what does the church believe?" "They believe what I believe?" They don't have much of a basis...I think it's real important to have the congregation grounded in scripture. I think a lot of pastors don't do that. They give a lot of feel-good stories, but they're not grounded. I think that's the primary purpose of preaching–that they're grounded to know why you believe what you believe. Somebody comes along telling them, "You don't have to believe in the resurrection." Then the congregation needs to know why we believe in the resurrection, why the bodily resurrection is important. Every now and then the preacher needs to preach on that and some of the core issues.

This emphasis on knowing what you believe has been of direct help to this listener. This person lost a spouse to leukemia about fifteen years ago (when the listener was about forty years old) and having a "grounded faith" was an enormous resource for facing the questions, pain, and loss of that season of life. "I had something to count on."

Thinking about the role of the Bible in preaching, a listener concludes that the preacher is to use the Bible "to teach us what God wants us to learn." For this person:

The Bible is kind of like a history book. It tells you what happened, why it happened, and what the outcome was for the circumstances of what people in Bible times did. I think that's for us–kind of giving us a warning as do parents. Instead of just saying like sometimes you tell a child, "Well, you just go do this." If they ask why, some people just say, "Because I said to do it. I'm the parent, so you have to do it." Sometimes I have heard parenting experts say you can't just do that. You have to give them the reasoning why. It's not just "I'm the authority and you're the unauthority person." I don't think God deals in that. That might not be the best way of parenting. A lot of times it's God using us as children and God didn't do that, say, "Well, these are the rules and that's that," and leave it that way. God gives us stories and lessons and says, "This is why I'm saying this. This is why you should do this, because if you don't, this is what can happen."

From this person's perspective, the preacher is a provocateur. "I think you have to have somebody up there that is trying to get your thoughts provoked, getting you to think for yourself, because we have to if we want it to be our own decision to believe what we believe instead of somebody saying this is what you must believe." This image is striking and very important for people on logos settings: the preacher provokes thought.

A highly educated member of a congregation says that preaching "grabs people's attention and grabs people's intellects in a way that nothing else does." The interviewer probes, "What about the sermon does that?" The listener responds, "Obviously different people are going to give different answers. That's why you're talking to a lot of people. I think that identifying a very solid specific thing and exploring it, with a good solid point to be made or points to be made, can do a lot to dilute distraction."

Several people with logos mindsets say that they joined particular congregations because those communities foster thinking about ideas that are significant to the listeners or because the beliefs of the denomination are intellectually satisfying. The members of a household who had been members in another denomination report their initial visit to the congregation where they have attended for several years. "The first sermon we heard—the first words out of the preacher's mouth were, 'Don't park your brain at the back door. God expects you to think. That's why God gave you freedom of choice and why God gave you a brain.' I decided that was where we wanted to be."

Another person tells the story of going from denomination to denomination, and then arriving at the present church home. "I was impressed with [the name of denomination] system, the theology, the way they did church." The church's doctrine (and hearing it interpreted from the pulpit in an "open-minded, non-dogmatic approach") was the attraction for this listener to join the congregation.

Ideas Affect These Listeners

Many people who listen to the sermon through logos settings say that they are changed by ideas. As a result of encountering important ideas, they shift their perspectives. Not only do they interpret the world differently, but they change their behavior. Not surprisingly, they also say that congregations change as a result of ideas that congregations accept.

According to a hearer who has talked extensively about the importance of the sermon in "clarifying issues," the sermon

> gives you God's word. I think it prepares you to go out into the world and do some of the things they talk about. In other words they're preparing you to make decisions in the world...When you leave, those things prepare you well to go out in the world and do justice.

In order to act in the world, this listener needs to have a clear grasp of the issues involved.

Some listeners have difficulty recalling particular sermons, but are still aware that ideas in preaching do have particular consequences.

> If you were to ask me any particular sermon and relate it back, I couldn't tell you. But I know I've walked out of sermons saying I need to be more patient with my kids. I need to probably think

things through better. Conscience-wise is there something that maybe I should be doing that I haven't done?…When you say stuff like that to me, it's, you know what? I haven't spent enough time with my kids, and I need to think more about doing that. I need to think about it because A, B, C, and that if I don't spend more time with them, this is what the end result might be.

This person, who comes to worship to learn from the sermon, hopes that the sermon will supply the ABCs, the rationale for specific actions.

Some persons interviewed for this project can recall specific sermons and/or specific effects.

I'm sure there have been effects as a result of the sermon. They encourage people to do things like participate in the Pride Parade here once a year which is for the gay/lesbian cause. Getting to the fairness campaign at election time which is to bar discrimination. We're big on the gay/lesbian thing because we're the only church in the area that will openly say something about it.

Elsewhere in the interview this person stresses the importance of the sermon in "making you think," and notes that theological ideas articulated in the pulpit prompt actions.

A person of non-Hispanic European origin in a congregation of similar people describes participating in a neighborhood outreach as a result of hearing it discussed in a sermon, and then illumines why the listeners responded to that sermon (and to other sermons that have prompted similar responses).

I remember sermons here at [name of congregation] that spoke to specific programs that were going on in [our city] to help, I'm going to say, problems in the neighborhood whether it be cleaning out crack houses. There's a black congregation across town that had purchased six or seven homes around the church and were asking for volunteers to come in and clean up yards and clean them. The sermon spoke to—was not a scolding sermon. It was a sermon of, "Here's an opportunity. The choice is yours. You can sit back or you can pick up the phone and call the person coordinating the effort who will tell you where to go and what to do." We had a great turnout.

The interviewer asks what the pastor did in the sermon to prompt such a response.

I think it was, "Here are certain problems," but it wasn't, "Here are these problems. Let's all pray." It also wasn't "Here are all these problems. Hey, upper-middle-class white [name of city], it's your fault." It was very much, "Here are these problems. Here are some opportunities. It's up to you. I want to encourage you to think about these." It's so much better than being scolded into something or being embarrassed into something, or being berated into something.

For this listener, thinking not only changes a person's point of view, but results in people taking direct actions.

A preacher, then, should give careful consideration to the kind of congregation that the preacher believes is most appropriate to the gospel. The preacher also needs to take into account the context in which the congregation finds itself. What kind of congregation is required for faithful witness in the setting in that congregation's context? What kind of preaching is likely to grow that kind of congregation? Furthermore, the preacher who seeks to affect persons who listen to the sermon through logos settings can do so through the use of ideas that the congregation perceives as important and that provide a rationale for why the congregation should adopt the claims of the sermon or should act in the way the congregation suggests.

Unfold the Ideas in an Orderly Way

None of the questions asked in the interviews focused specifically on sermon form or style. Nevertheless, many auditors of sermons on logos settings state explicitly that they like for the sermon to unfold in orderly ways. Some of these members of local communities listen for the sermon to make a single major "point" or to offer multiple "points," that is, straightforward ideas about God and the world that the congregation can take seriously. Given the caricature of sermons in a previous era as "three points and a poem," it is worth noting that even among those who listen for points, there is little expectation that a sermon should always have three points. Indeed, only a handful of persons interviewed characterized the sermon as having three points. Congregants who listen on logos settings, however, do have a driving desire to get the message in a clear and straightforward way.

The following remark summarizes a strain that is common to many interviews in this cohort. Developing the idea that a sermon must be well-constructed and have a definite flow or movement, a hearer says:

> The sermon has to be good public speaking. I am a scientist. I've done public speaking. I connect well with having things well prepared. I have no tolerance for things that are ill presented. I just have no tolerance for it. So it needs to have a thought progression where I can see and hear the stories being told and what points are being made, how they fit together. If I pay attention well enough, I should understand by the end how it relates to the beginning and that there was a thought process involved. I need to see the logic. I need to see the flow.

Another person identifies "organization" as an important characteristic of an engaging sermon. "I think the organization of the sermon is ninety percent of it. It has to be organized before you can really present it and really reach to meet the objectives of that particular sermon."

Many persons who hear the sermon in logos ways are content with only one point. "I want to take one idea home with me that I can use." Whether a sermon has one point or several, or whether the points are identified as such, are matters that are secondary to the concern of these hearers to pick up the major claims of the sermon and to interact with it.

Another listener poignantly describes the consequences of a sermon by a guest minister that suffered from lack of discipline:

> There was a time, and it wasn't very long ago, when we had a guest preacher and it was absolutely horrible. I'm used to orderly, structured listening, and going somewhere. This person rambled and was everywhere, and I was so exhausted. I was so tired trying to hear, "What are you trying to say?" So that just made me very tired and I thought, "Please don't bring that person back here anymore."

This latter attitude is a like a refrain among people who listen to the sermon through logos settings. When the sermon is not cogent, they resist paying attention.

Some of these hearers even make direct suggestions about how to arrange sermons to facilitate listening:

> Keep it short. Say, you've got fifteen minutes. There's got to be something that grabs everybody's attention. If, in the first two or three minutes of that fifteen minutes, you get people to think—you stimulate their thoughts—I think they'll tend to listen more through the rest of the sermon. If it starts off kind of dull, or there's no consistency or continuity in what's being said, I think people turn off and tend not to listen. That's happened sometimes.

Unfortunately, this person does not give an example of the kind of beginning that "gets people to think." Another listener warms to sermons in which the preacher says, at the beginning, "Three points and I'll be through."

> That's pretty effective primarily because there's an opening, a middle, and a conclusion. Much more than three points? Come on. How much am I going to comprehend about this? It gives the pastor too much of an opportunity to wander. So those are usually pretty good. Sometimes one point sermons are pretty good, so long as they focus and not try to cover too much ground. Those are always effective.

Another listener recalls a former minister, who was very effective. That minister was

> great at signposting. That minister would say, "We're going to cover three points." That minister would say, "Number one is…Number two is…Number three is." The former minister was very clear at the beginning about, "Today we're going to talk about three issues relating to…" That was very helpful in following along, and it also kind of gave you an idea how hard the minister worked on the sermon. I like that kind of outline so I can follow along.

A different kind of sermon comes to mind:

> A contrast of that would be what we experienced in [another congregation in another city] where the minister used sort of a stream of consciousness approach where the minister just started and went, and you had no idea where it was going to end up. When it ended, you were surprised because, "Oh is that the end? Was that the conclusion? Are we done? Is there more coming?"

Many of these listeners find sermons with "surprise endings" to be unsatisfactory. The congregation gets to the big idea but isn't given much help figuring out what to do with it.

We interviewed in only a couple of congregations in which the preaching is supplemented by an overhead projector or PowerPoint presentation. The listeners in one of these congregations expressed appreciation for the fact that the points of the sermon are nearly always identified on the screen. In a few other congregations the pastor provides an outline of the sermon in the bulletin, about which one person says, "It just makes it easier having the outline in the bulletin for people who like to do that. I do that some. I'll take it back home."

Appreciation of Comparison and Contrast of Different Viewpoints

Another distinctive note among many folk who approach the sermon via logos settings is appreciation for the preacher alerting them to the different ways that issues can be interpreted and to helping them compare and contrast the options for interpretation. Appreciation for balanced presentation of ideas and issues is found in interviewees from congregations located along the theological spectrum from liberal to conservative.[8] While some perspectives are voiced in response to questions about preaching on potentially explosive issues, they also appear when interviewees are asked about other things.

After noting impatience with sermons focusing on the negative things that a person should not do, a listener from a congregation with a liberal spirit nuances:

Just as I dislike being told what not to do, telling me things that I can't do that are being bad, I don't like being told what to do either. I much prefer to think that through myself and make my own choices and decisions. Sermons that help me make choices and decisions that are good decisions, they engage me.

Another listener says, with appreciation, "I think the preacher takes a lot of current issues and gives us various ways to look at them. It isn't all right or wrong, but helps us look at the different facets of an issue." This approach, according to this congregant, impacts both individuals and the community, and helps shape the congregation to do the same. The congregation itself now approaches issues in the same fashion (as can be heard in "sharing sessions" after the sermon). A number of listeners who receive the sermon through logos settings voice similar thought: They are drawn to sermons that help them think through issues.

A hearer from a congregation with a conservative theological worldview makes a similar point when recollecting, with considerable detail, a particular sermon.

> I remember one example in particular. The senior minister stood up and said, "I would like to tell you that drinking is wrong. There would be nothing more that I would love to do than stand in this pulpit and say that it is a sin to have a glass of wine. But the Bible doesn't say that. Now let me tell you all the reasons why I think you should abstain, and why I personally abstain. But the Bible doesn't say. This is what I've chosen to do and where I'm comfortable. It says if I should cause anyone else to stumble, then that's a sin. Therefore, I feel like if I personally engage in this activity, I may cause someone else to stumble. So, therefore…"

This listener (like many others) wants to know the preacher's interpretation, but is likely to be less suspicious and more willing to engage it when it is identified as the preacher's interpretation.

In response to the question of whether there are issues that are too explosive for the pulpit, another listener offers specific examples while approving of how the senior minister handles not only sermons that are potentially explosive, but a wide range of issues that are complex and even ambiguous. "The minister will lay out the facts before you and give you the opportunity to finish the story, if you will, for yourself." An example comes to mind:

> At our previous church, probably the most explosive issue was concerning having women ministers. It was still [in the same denomination], but was very fundamental in reading through the scriptures and saying "No, it is not biblical for there to be a woman senior minister. That just isn't right." So issues like that could have

been explosive for the church if the minister is coming and saying, "This is right," or "This is wrong." It tends to be more divisive than a minister who would come and say, "Here are the facts. Here are the positives of it. Here are the negatives of it as I understand them. Now you need to really deal with these two sets of facts and come out with a conclusion."

Another example comes to mind that reflects the fact that the interview took place a few weeks after the destruction of the World Trade Towers in September, 2001.

I have struggled recently, with, again, in our discussions nationally of retaliation against Osama Bin Laden, and perhaps using military action against Afghanistan. I, as a human say, "Go get them. Let's bomb them off the face of the earth." I, as a Christian, have to say, "Jesus said, 'Turn the other cheek.'" What good will it do for us to go over and take 10,000, 20,000, or 50,000 innocent lives? What good did it do for us over in Hiroshima to kill whatever it was, 75,000 in the first day, or something like that, by dropping the A-bomb. What does that accomplish to our Christian mission? What's explosive? What's not explosive? What is a watered-down sermon versus letting you make your own decisions? It's a tough call, a real tough call. There certainly needs to be enough guidance to keep a congregation true to the beliefs of their religions, of Christianity. Certainly there are differences between Baptists, Methodists, Presbyterians, and I think a church should be true to those beliefs of their individual denomination. Beyond that, great sermons stimulate people to make their own decisions on controversial, explosive types of issues.

Although this listener shows a preference for individual critical thinking, the listener is not awash in individualism and relativity; decisions should be measured against the beliefs of the community (a logos concern). Elsewhere in the interview, this listener indicates that ministers can certainly express their own conclusions about issues but should do so by sharing with the congregation the reasons for those conclusions (and pointing out the weak points).

Several persons who appreciate this spirit of critical reflection also have reservations. "Now let me hasten to add," says one, "that there's a danger there of watering down a message by simply laying the plusses and minuses out there and saying, 'Now it's up to you to determine what you should be doing.'" On theological grounds, many preachers will rightly resist the idea that all the preacher does is offer people a cafeteria line of opinions from which they select their own interpretations. However, a preacher can take advantage of the critical mood with which many persons listen to the sermon through logos settings by acknowledging other possibilities for interpretation even while articulating what the preacher considers a normative one.

The Preacher Needs to be Prepared

Not surprisingly, the listeners who are the focus of this chapter say more about their desire to know that the preacher is prepared than do representatives from ethos and pathos groups. Preachers can signal they are prepared by developing the sermon in such a way that people have the sense that they are going in a definite direction and by referring, in the sermon itself, to research, wrestling with issues, and other aspects of preparation.

The following remark names qualities in preparation and presentation that many listeners who receive the sermon on process settings find attractive:

> The preachers in the congregation are so well read and so knowledgeable and so up-to-date on current events and history and literature and philosophy. When someone can bring to a sermon, first of all, a relationship with God…and Jesus Christ…and base a sermon primarily on the revelation of God through scripture, but add to that literature and history and classic culture and philosophy, it really is a great experience intellectually, not only spiritually, but intellectually.

Still another listener hopes that the preacher will use "seminary teachings" in a full- bodied way in the sermon. In a similar way, when commenting on good preachers, a listener goes further.

> I think that the one common thread among good preachers is that not only are they well educated, but they continue to be educated. I think that some people forget their studenting skills, but a really good pastor maintains studenting skills and then shares. I think that enables them to be more effective teachers. I put that very, very high on my list.

Many of these listeners regard education as essential to effective preaching.

Describing developments in the congregation, a long-time member of a mega church makes a significant suggestion to increase the amount of time that preachers can devote to the sermon:

> I will tell you, and probably you will hear this from people here. The one thing that, to their benefit, the preaching ministers have is that they have a lot of time to prepare their messages. The senior minister will spend, this minister will tell you, thirty to thirty-five hours a week. You can't do that in small churches because you

have so many other demands on your time. It took a lot to educate our membership that, if the senior minister didn't show up for every funeral and every time a member went into the hospital, that was okay. The members were probably going to be better served if someone else did some of that because the senior minister probably couldn't spend the time with you that someone else could. That is a member education process, particularly with smaller congregations. I think that the lay people should be doing many of those things, to allow the minister, or whoever's going to be delivering the message Sundays…that you cannot possibly do that in an effective way if you do not have time to do it.

Some ministers, of course, will object that being present with members in the hospital and at other significant events is at the heart of their understanding of ministry. Such concerns should not obscure the larger value of this listener's perspective–that ministers do not always need to be the ones to perform the full range of tasks expected of them and that lay people are often better qualified to do some of the responsibilities that ministers routinely carry out. Indeed, involving lay leaders at such levels can be a way of enacting the priesthood of all believers.

The preacher's preparation in the study (and other places) does not exclude the work of the Holy Spirit. According to a thoughtful parishioner, the Holy Spirit "gives the preacher the ability to prepare the sermon."

Logos Settings Interact with Ethos

As noted previously, a person who takes in the sermon through logos settings also is affected by ethos and pathos settings. People who approach the sermon through logos settings frequently interpret ethos and pathos concerns in relationship to logos in manners that range from ways assumed by traditional rhetoric to those for whom the character of the preacher seems unrelated to the truthfulness of the content. Furthermore, these listeners view relationships from the perspective of understanding–both of how relationships help them understand the gospel and how the gospel helps them understand relationships.

Traditional Ethos Associations Refracted through Logos

Traditional ethos associations come to expression in the following remarks. Note, however, that the listeners speak of these concerns in relationship to logos. In the first case, a listener answers, "When does a sermon have authority for you?"

When I feel like the person who's speaking it is a genuine person, and it's clear that there's some thought behind it, and it's well constructed and put together. I'm very keen on the presentation of sermons, and if I don't feel like the person is genuine, or if it just seems like spitting things out without much thought behind it, then I don't give much credence to that. I lose interest and faith in that topic pretty quickly.

When the preacher does not seem to be genuine, the respondent is reluctant to invest in the sermon. However, for this respondent the preacher "being a genuine person" is insufficient reason for trying to pay attention to the sermon. The sermon must have "some thought behind it."

The next remark is reminiscent of the previous one as the interviewee describes a good preacher.

Somebody who's open to you and who's willing to listen to what you think and not be…too demanding that you believe just exactly like they do and who are willing to accept people who have different ideas. But a good preacher demonstrates what I consider Christians should be like, somebody who accepts people without being extremely judgmental. Who also is, I guess, scholarly in their approach towards their sermons, and being able to evoke thought-provoking type sermons that get you to thinking…I like somebody who can evoke thoughtful responses to you and get your mind thinking about Christ and religion in general and being able to keep you throughout the week thinking about what they said.

The ethos concerns of perceiving the preacher as person who is open, accepting, and willing to listen are also characteristics that this listener values in the content of the sermon that the listener mentions here and at other points in the interview–thought- provoking, open to fresh ideas, and someone who brings "a rational approach to understanding the deeper meanings of some of the things said in the Bible."

Message Takes Priority over Messenger

The logos emphasis is even higher on the following excerpts from transcripts in which the interviewees say that the content of the message is of much greater value than their perception of the character of (or relationship with) the messenger. The language of message and messenger is suggested by an interviewee who recalled sermons that had proven very helpful in their affirmation of the providence of God in the midst of difficult situations. The interviewer asks, "Was that more about the message that connected with you, or was it the messenger?" This person replies, "I think it was the message."

This theme is expressed with more force by other listeners, such as this report from a member of a megachurch in which this listener does not have a close personal relationship with the senior minister, but does with some of the associate pastors.

Here at [name of congregation] I know the associate ministers pretty well because I've worked on the [name of] Committee with them. I was good friends with a previous associate minister and another previous associate minister, and when they preach, I don't think it makes much difference to me that I know them better than I know the current senior minister.

This listener then sounds the theme of this group of folk in the study. "It's what they have to say."

A member of a congregation recalls a minister with whom this person had a distant, even contentious, relationship. The interviewer wants to know if listening to that pastor's sermons was "different for you as a result of not having that close relationship."

No. I've come to believe in sanctification. There is something about the pulpit and putting yourself under it. The identity of the preacher really doesn't matter. If I didn't want to be distracted, I could close my eyes and listen, but what was coming from there was not coming from the preacher really. It was coming from God. I guess I believe that, and I guess I experience that, and understand that. What I hear and what I get, I'm supposed to get. The vessel and the vehicle don't make that much difference.

For this listener, the preached word has a life and power of its own that operates almost independently of the person who speaks it.

Another listener perceptively points out that good character is not itself a guarantee of a trustworthy message. People of good character can think incorrectly.

I think that if the character of the preacher makes a difference, the difference is small. The difference might be in my perhaps going in with a sense of receptiveness, but there are people whom I have really liked who have presented really flawed, well-intentioned sermons. There are people, frankly, who I have really struggled with as individuals. There are some in our church. Okay? Who have spoken from the pulpit and explored a theme or something very, very well. Maybe this is just me, but for me, I'm capable of stepping away from that. In fact, sometimes it's better because it's always more disappointing to me when somebody I really like gets up and doesn't fulfill that promise...If somebody gets up to speak I don't care for, I may be a little grumpy at the beginning, but I'll lay that aside.

For theater-goers, "The play's the thing." Something similar is true for these. The message is the thing.

Relationship as Means to Understanding

For people who listen to sermons on logos settings, relationship (and perception of relationship) is often important because these listeners view relationships (or perception of relationships) from the perspective of understanding—both of how relationships help them understand the major ideas of the sermon and how the major ideas of the sermon inform their understanding of relationship. The same thing is frequently true of material in the sermon that comes from the preacher's personal experience or stories and illustrations in which the congregation identifies with a character or an aspect of the setting or plot. Listeners who hear the sermon through ethos settings often approach these matters of ethos through the lens of how a relationship illumines (or frustrates) their awareness of the message of the sermon. The focus is on understanding, a distinctively logos concern.

We notice these themes in a listener's answer to the question "What do you think pastors are doing when they preach?"

> That's an interesting question. What do I think they're trying to do? I would think they're trying to lead us to a better understanding of who God is. Trying to help us see more clearly what our role is here on earth. What is it that God would have us do? Helping us to understand God's will for our lives in general. Helping us to know ourselves better. Helping us to understand each other better. Helping us to foster peace in our relationships. Making a world a better place. Trying to facilitate community and fellowship and love. I think those are the things that God would have us do. That's what a pastor is like—a shepherd who is guiding the flock.

Note how the logos language of "knowing" and "understanding" permeates this interview. When this listener speaks about the purpose of preaching, the listener interprets ethos aspects (e.g., relating to the world on earth, understanding one another) from the standpoint of logos (a better understanding of who God is).

A listener speaks about the use of the preacher's personal experience or a story from another source as functioning much like evidence in a courtroom. "Give me the evidence. I'm listening. I'll hear you. Give me a story. Give me your personal experience. I'll take it into consideration." For this hearer, the content of the personal experience or story explicitly serves to persuade (or not persuade, as the case may be).

A listener who is asked to identify the most important thing that happens in the congregation initially answers with the one word, "Community," but then explains community in logos terms. "I'm able to get together with other people that believe the same way." Preaching in this medium-size congregation functions as teaching. The listener says that the minister is "a good pastor, much better speaker, more so than interpersonal relationships,

so we talk, shake hands every once in a while, but nothing real personal."
The sermon challenges people to "think and learn" which shapes the
congregation as community. "The congregation can be molded on what
the preacher preaches. People hear, because you get people hearing the
same sermon. If they're not enjoying it or not liking it, they're going to go
some place else. So I think the sermon helps mold the congregation." This
listener believes that the teaching quality of the sermon (logos) shapes the
character of the community.

A few people who follow the sermon on logos go a step further. Asked
to talk a little bit about the relationships a listener has had with preachers,
a listener says:

> We've had some good pastors. When I say "good," they were really
> into preaching the word and really gave an account of what the
> Bible was saying in ways that we could understand. Then we had
> ministers that didn't preach the word at all, just got up there and
> talked about boys needing to keep their zippers up and girls needing
> to keep their dresses down, and not really touching anything
> concerning the Bible. Now that was very, very boring and a big
> turn-off. But now, our present minister is really into the word.
> This minister is into change. This minister has accepted change,
> and is not back in the old-fogey days. This minister really speaks
> about what the people need to hear and about things that are going
> on now. I think we enjoy that.

This person's response to the content of the sermon is almost
synonymous with the person's perception of relationship with the pastor.

Logos Settings Interact with Pathos

People who listen to the sermon through logos settings are affected by
pathos. Some of the interviewee responses to the role of pathos in their
response to the sermon follow closely the functions set out by traditional
rhetoric. However, as in the case of the interaction of logos and ethos just
discussed, these listeners often interpret pathos emphases in relationship
to qualities of listening characteristic of logos. Some of the people in this
listening cohort distrust emotion. For many others, an experience of feeling
may enhance their perception of the event of preaching, especially when
an emotion is a response to information or ideas in the sermon. For some
of these listeners, the logos setting is lower than for others while the pathos
setting is higher, and they speak positively of being moved by pathos.
However, the presence of pathos is not essential for these listeners. For
some, the experience of feeling should prompt reflection. What do these
feelings mean? Often when these listeners describe moments of pathos in
the sermon (or the effects of pathos in individual or corporate settings),
they use the language of logos, that is, of understanding, thought, and

meaning. Indeed, many of these listeners seek an intellectual interpretation of the meaning of the feelings that they experience in preaching and elsewhere in life. They want to be able to name what they feel.

Traditional Functions of Pathos in Logos Settings

For some of the folk who take in the sermon through logos settings, pathos functions to increase the receptivity of the hearer to the content of the sermon. This theme is alive even in listeners who have some reservations about the role of pathos in responding to the sermon. The following listener described a sermon in which the preacher spoke tenderly and poignantly, in the midst of a sermon on Job, about the death of the minister's child. The interviewer asks, "Were you stirred emotionally by that?"

> Yes. I was stirred emotionally by that, and emotion is not something I normally think of as real desirable in a sermon. I would much prefer intellectual rigor over an emotional response, but in this case, the preacher had very carefully talked about Job. The minister laid out the scripture verses, talked about the issues, and then at the end, pulled it all together with the minister's own personal experience. It was inspirational. It wasn't maudlin, and it was moving. That was a very good balance in that sermon between dealing with difficult theological issues, but then having the emotional element that kind of brought it all home. What I don't like is if emotion seems to be for emotion's sake. Everybody say, "Hallelujah. Again. Hallelujah, hallelujah." There's no content there. It's just a fervor that doesn't have anything to support it. But in this case, where the preacher had laid out everything so well and used an emotional element at the end to sort of close the sermon and bring it all together, it was a powerful tool.

For this person, pathos (feeling) has a utilitarian character: It is "a powerful tool." The preacher, from this perspective, adds emotional material to the sermon to help create an environment in the sermon in which the listener is as receptive as possible to the big ideas of the sermon.

Another listener notices that telling stories is a primary way that preachers stir both individuals and communities.

> Well, stories have a primary place. There's no doubt about that. Being a member of a profession that requires a lot of public speaking, I'm aware of what holds the attention of the people you're speaking to, and stories and anecdotes are really necessary in a sermon to focus people's attention, to get people thinking about themselves, applying the sermon to their own lives. There's really nothing like a good story to bring home the message. I don't enjoy sermons that are primarily anecdotes and stories strung together,

but I don't downplay the importance of anecdotes and stories and things like that. I think they're of primary importance and almost a necessary place in the sermon.

Here we hear classical reason for including material in speeches and sermons that generate pathos: to hold attention, to "bring home the message." Logos concerns come to the surface, too: "to get people thinking about themselves" and "applying" the sermon.

Low Awareness of Feeling

A significant number of people who fall into the category of listening to the sermon in logos ways describe themselves with lines like the following:[9]

> Many times after church, I say a little prayer. I'm thankful to be able to attend worship services. Then, hopefully, I'll be able to put into effect some of the things the pastor talked about. I guess I'm just not an emotional person. I'm not a person who cries a lot. Of course, I'm not an "Amen" type of person either. I hear the sermon and I get a lot out of it, but I'm not emotionally carried away.

Another comment from another interviewee is similar:

> I'm motivated without it getting to my feelings. That's just me. I don't need somebody to be up in tears with a shaky voice and trembling kind of thing. I'm not saying it's wrong if somebody does that occasionally. That's just not something I need or that particularly makes me feel better or pulls me closer to God.

Similar comments run through many interviews with logos-leaning listeners. "I am not an emotional person." "I do not have a great many feelings about anything." "I don't go up or down much." "I am not affected by feelings." "I'm not one that's generally touched by emotions."

A related question moved into the congregational arena. "I would like for you to describe a sermon that seemed to move the congregation as a whole, as a community." Again, the handful of listeners who think of themselves as not aware of (or not affected by) emotion could not remember a sermon when the congregation as a whole was moved. For instance, one listener says, simply, "Not specifically."[10] After pondering a moment, the person continues, "I think there probably have. I can't remember" [another pause]. "Well, if we go way back outside this church, I can do that." The listener (who is now a little over fifty years old) remembers a sermon from age ten in a revival meeting in a congregation in the South. The listener thinks of that sermon from years ago as "old-fashioned" from an "uneducated" preacher with "no training." In that culture, "The minister is expected to work up to this emotional level." The listener then recounts the emotional reaction to the "hellfire and brimstone" sermon. "That [listening to the sermon] was uncomfortable not because it made me feel like I was not going necessarily to hell, but because I wished for home." Two things are interesting in this response. One is that other interviewees from the same congregation *could* identify occasions when the congregation was moved. This interviewee has evidently been unaware of such responses in the worshipping community. The other interesting thing is that the emotion stirred in the interviewee by the sermon at the revival was discomfort with the emotional quality of the preaching itself, emanating in the desire to flee the meeting and to return home. The listener says, wistfully, of that early experience. "I wish I had attended another church" (presumably one with less emotional preaching).

Distrust of Feeling

A significant number of people who track the sermon on logos settings go beyond not noticing emotions. They distrust feeling as bases for understanding life and for making major decisions. Many in this group make explicit statements indicating the superiority of intellectual content— such as information, ideas, arguments, assessment of strengths and weaknesses—for determining the meaning of life and for making decisions.

A person interviewed for the study says plainly, "Your emotions will lie to you." This person does think emotion can have a place in preaching. "Some emotion, yes. But this where you get people so wound up, so stirred up. That's what these preachers do. The ones that run around and jump around and all that kind of stuff. They get people so wound up." Too much emotion (or the wrong kind of emotion) can obscure the point of hearing a sermon. "You need that teaching." The listener confirms, "It kind of goes back to what you expect in life to some extent. The preaching life is not necessarily all fun and games. It's more of a challenge than that in my view. I think some of that emotion sometimes is just this rah-rah, everything is going to be all right, and ultimately it will be, but in this situation, God may be really wanting to bring something out of you."

Several people in the study group join the previous listener in observing that the effects of emotional responses to the sermon are short-lived. A listener says, "I don't look for sermons to motivate me." The interviewer asks what this listener does look for sermons to do.

> To challenge me. To give me insight. To cause me to pause about my beliefs. Maybe I'm too rigid in this area, but I want the sermon to cause me to pause and say maybe I need to listen more to God's word. But this is not to motivate me, to fire me up. I'm not into motivational speakers although I listened to them when I was in sales. To me it was a waste of time. Yes, it pumps you up. So what? Two weeks later you are back where you were. So you got a little

boost. You went back...What are you expecting from your pastor?...It's a matter of self-discipline. God is giving us power through the Holy Spirit and we should have self-discipline. I don't need a motivational speech. I need discipline. It's nice to have an encouraging word, but you don't win the Olympics by hearing a motivational speech. You win the Olympics from discipline.

As other comments in the interview make clear, the discipline to which this listener refers is getting solid ideas about God and the world that are animated by the Holy Spirit.

Reliving a sermon on a sensitive issue, a listener moves from describing how the preacher framed the issue to help minimize an emotional response that might have distracted the congregation from considering the issue as issue, to a general observation about how preachers might handle such matters.

I think something that was potentially emotional the preacher approached in a very professional way, in a very academic way, respecting that there was an emotional aspect to it; but approached it in a very academic kind of way that I think encouraged the audience, the congregation, to step away from that emotional response...Again, that goes back to treating your congregation as adults and recognizing the intellect of the congregation. When we talk about explosive topics, we usually mean social issues, but I think the historical Jesus movement which the preacher had discussed in a recent sermon is something that is potentially upsetting to a lot of people.

For this listener, feeling can get in the way of thinking clearly about important issues. The hearer thinks that a relatively detached ("academic") approach to an issue minimizes the threat of emotion clouding the congregation's consideration of an issue.

Some listeners who hear the sermon through logos settings think that emotion can work against some of the purposes of preaching. A hearer makes such a comment:

But I guess on the down side of that [a celebration in the latter stages of the sermon], sometimes you get that large emotional response to a sermon, you can lose some of the effectiveness, whereas you're not hearing what is actually said because you're still caught up in that emotional high.

The problem, for this person, is that pathos obscures "what is actually said." A similar concern is heard from a listener of non-Hispanic European origin. The interviewer asks if the respondent can think of a time when the congregation as a whole was stirred.

Yes. Not in an overly zealous way, like I've been to some other church cultures where emotions really do take off. To be frank, they sometimes get a little too noisy. That usually makes me uncomfortable when it gets too noisy. I feel that's how God gets sometimes lost. When things get too overly emotional, I think we tend to lose focus and tend to focus more on our experience and elevate ourselves above why we're here.

These listeners are concerned not about emotion itself (about which they both speak positively) but about excesses that interfere with the purposes of worship and preaching, which they perceive as being the communication of content (logos).

Pathos Should Prompt Reflection

Many of the listeners who hear the sermon through logos settings believe that the presence of pathos in response to the sermon calls for reflection that tries to state clearly what the feeling may or may not mean, and how it relates to the message of the sermon. Even when these folk appreciate ideas leading to a deep sense of being moved, the experience of being stirred is insufficient, by itself, to be the basis for determining meaning or making major life choices.

The following remark both summarizes the uneasiness of many people who hear the sermon through logos perspectives with aspects of pathos, and indirectly suggests what emotion should do in a sermon. This listener is asked to remember a sermon that stirred the emotions of the whole congregation.

I can't. Our minister is not that kind of preacher...It's more a kind of quiet, thoughtful process...rather than play on emotions. Emotions tend to be a bit unreliable, I think, and fickle. They're great for the moment. I've seen preachers who are quite dramatic and can make you laugh and cry, but how long does that last for? I don't know. It's fine at the time, but has it left you with anything that you can reflect on? Maybe not.

This recognizes that emotions can be quite powerful, but is suspicious of their long-lasting effects. The sermon, for this hearer, needs to leave the congregation with something "you can *reflect* on." When pathos occurs in a sermon, it should, for this listener, serve a logos purpose: create an experience that the listener can think about. Several other listeners recount sermons in which experiences of pathos in the sermon itself have led them to fresh understanding.

A similar motif recurs in the following response to the interviewer's request to recall a sermon that moved this person. The listener recalls a sermon mentioned earlier in this book—when the pastor pulled two large chairs into the chancel and interviewed the former moderator of the congregation, whose spouse was dying from cancer.

> I would go back to the period in time when the senior pastor did a series on intercessory prayer. That series was interrupted with a Sunday when the pastor dialogued with the husband of the woman who ultimately passed away here a couple of weeks ago. That was captivating. To hear someone who was facing the death of his wife get up and say, "But I know that my God loves me. I don't hold this against God. I'm not angry about it. It's a fact of life that ultimately we die. Now we don't like to let people go, but ultimately it's a fact of life that those we love pass on to be with God."

The interviewer goes on, "Can you say what in that sermon particularly stirred you?"

> I think certainly it was the openness. There wasn't anything in that sermon that I felt as made up, that was necessarily rehearsed of "This is the way I need to say this particularly... This is the way I need to respond to this particular question." Now, I'm sure that the former moderator probably knew what the questions were ahead so as to give some thought to them. We have considered this couple to be good friends over the past five or six years. It certainly was an opportunity for anyone who considered them as friends, as well as brothers and sisters in Christ, to really bond with the former moderator in lifting that person up. Just giving a hug, a handshake, a whatever. It was an opportunity for us to really reflect on our own lives and say, "Wow. And we think we have troubles sometimes." We know nothing of what this person is going through. I think it was a real time for a bonding of the congregation.

These comments illustrate the interweaving of settings in a single person. The sermon generates feelings (pathos) that lead to bonding between the congregation and the former moderator. In terms of logos, the payoff is that the sermon prompted the congregation "to really reflect on our own lives."

Another listener notes that moments in sermons that leave the listener feeling badly can actually serve the greater logos good.

> The two ministers I've experienced here are excellent. So you always expect to get a meaningful sermon. I think we've been fortunate that we've had the two ministers because their sermons were very stimulating and challenging. They are not sermons that make you feel good. They are sermons that may make you feel more or less inadequate. That's why I look forward to Sundays.

For this listener, the feeling of inadequacy generated by the sermon is a prime opportunity for the mind to be stimulated. It is more important for the sermon to challenge this listener in a significant way than to encourage this listener to feel good.

At the end of a long discussion about the importance of dealing with potentially controversial issues from the pulpit—issues that could generate highly emotional responses—one member of a congregation posits a classic logos approach. "I think for any kind of issue, the more that the congregation understands it, the less divisive it becomes and the more they can come to a consensus of how to deal with it." From the perspective of this listener's setting, understanding (good information and ideas) creates the climate within which a congregation can deal with emotion.

Ideas Generate Feeling

The following statement is reminiscent of the previous one in revealing that encounter with significant intellectual content can create passion:

> The excitement of preaching God's word and the excitement of receiving God's word. Everything about God should be exciting. That's the way I see it. God was not a dull person saying you need to live a dull life and get up every morning, go to work, come home, see your spouse, talk to your kids, go to bed, get up. God is an exciting person...Talking about the good things that God does. To me, God's word is exciting, and the more I learn about it every day, it gets more and more exciting. That's one of the reasons why I like fellowship with other members, because you learn something every day.

Learning, for this listener, is directly related to excitement. The more the person learns the more excited this person becomes. Indeed, the respondent ties together logos, pathos and ethos by indicating that learning takes place both from the sermon and from fellowship with other members.

While the characteristics we have discussed in this chapter are associated with hearing sermons on logos settings, these characteristics are not found only among people who are inclined to logos. As we must constantly remember, many characteristics often identified with logos are found in differing degrees from one congregant to another among people who tune into the sermon on other settings. As we observed in the previous chapter, and will note again in the following one, people who enter sermons through ethos and pathos settings also show forth qualities that are frequently (but not only) identified with logos. However, the fact that a sizable number of people in the usual congregation hear the sermon on logos settings should push the preacher to put the following question to the sermon: "Am I including material to help engage listeners who hear the sermon through logos settings?"

CHAPTER 4

Pathos Settings

In the Introduction, we met Pat, a listener who remarked on how moving a sermon was. "I was on the verge of tears. I even had to get my handkerchief and wipe my eyes." When the preacher inquired what, in the sermon, seemed to touch Pat, the congregant replied, "It was the story you told about God's love for us, even when we do things that are not loving. Sometimes I feel so unlovely, but your story made me feel loved." For Pat, the presence of emotion in response to the sermon is a sign of the positive quality of the sermon. Pat responds to preaching through the ways it stirs feelings. Pat pays attention to the character of (and relationship with) the preacher, to information, and ideas, but sermons seem most compelling when Pat is moved emotionally.

Pat shares this approach to the sermon with many other people. The research informing the present book reveals that a significant percentage of people hear sermons through pathos settings.[1] These communicants typically feel that they have engaged a sermon seriously when a sermon stirs them emotionally in a positive way.

In this chapter, I first outline the characteristics of pathos in traditional rhetoric. The central part of the chapter turns to the interviews themselves to listen to persons who listen to the sermon on pathos settings. I report how they describe hearing sermons. I then take up ways that listeners on pathos settings interact with ethos and logos material. In connection with the different discussions in the chapter, I note things a preacher can do to enhance appeal to the person who hears the sermon through pathos.

Characteristics of Pathos in Rhetoric

According to rhetoricians, pathos is a multilayered phenomenon. As most obviously suggested by the word "pathos" itself, it has to do with the roles that feelings play in how an audience or congregation responds to a speech or sermon. "The orator persuades" when the members of an audience or congregation "are roused to emotions by" the speech or sermon. "For the judgments we deliver are the not the same when we are influenced by joy or sorrow, love or hate."[2] In a particular worship setting on a particular day, a listening community may be moved to accept the claims made by the speaker or preacher by the emotions that are stirred by the message. A speaker seeks to use pathos in such a way as to create a favorable disposition towards the claims of the speech in the sermon. A speaker using pathos sometimes tries to invoke emotions (and other associations) that directly relate to the content of the sermon. For instance, a preacher trying to persuade the congregation to love their neighbors could tell a poignant story about people loving their neighbors.

A congregation or audience may also be affected by feelings that have been stirred by things happening in the wider world, and these feelings may contribute to how the group responds to the public address or sermon. These factors beyond the congregation can help create an environment in which the listeners are favorably (or unfavorably) disposed towards what the speaker would like for them to think or do. A tornado in a neighboring community, for instance, may evoke a sense of empathy in the congregation for those who have lost homes in the nearby town.[3]

Lucy Lind Hogan and Robert Reid, rhetoricians and scholars of preaching who help preachers bring insights from rhetoric into the service of the sermon, perceptively call attention to the fact that, while listeners often take seriously "abstract, rational demonstrations" in making significant decisions and about what to believe and do, listeners also render "judgments in cumulative, associative, and practical ways." Listeners reach conclusions based not only on rational evidence and arguments that are tied directly to the issue at hand, but also on the basis of emotions, intuitions and wider associations that may be triggered by the issue or the sermon.[4]

Lind Hogan and Reid rightly press us to recognize when a speaker or preacher wants to change or reinforce the listeners' values or actions. The speech or sermon must do more than stir general feelings in the listeners. Pathos, when serving an optimum purpose in the sermon or speech, encourages the listeners to care about the ideas in the sermon and to act accordingly. Indeed, they write, "The most effective use of emotion in a speech occurs when it helps listeners understand why you, as the preacher, *care* in a way that helps them, as listeners, *care* as well."[5] These rhetoricians follow the legendary authority in rhetoric in the late twentieth century, Kenneth Burke, in asserting that people care when they identify with the speaker. Identification can involve both the conscious sense (on the part of listeners) that speaker and listener share a common cause as well as less conscious ways in which the audience identifies with the speaker.[6]

An individual or a group frequently adopts an idea or pursues a particular course of actions, in part, because of the feelings that are prompted by those ideas, images or actions. While such feelings and associations can be quite powerful, they may never rise to the level of consciousness. Over the course of the life of an individual or community the feelings and other associations with particular ideas or behaviors can change (again, sometimes without the person even becoming aware of it).

Listening to Listeners Who Hear the Sermon on Pathos Settings

For many listeners, pathos not only functions as described in classical rhetoric and a setting through which they hear the sermon, but is additionally a mode of knowledge that is activated by the sermon (and by associations evoked by the sermon). Pathos, feelings, can be released by material in the sermon, as well as by the community's perception of the persona of the preacher, and by associations evoked by events and other things outside the setting of worship and even outside the congregation.[7]

Feeling as a Mode of Knowledge

Many congregants who listen to the sermon through pathos settings are aware that emotion is important to them. Several speak plainly about this orientation in self-identifications such as the following. "I am a very emotional person." "I'm pretty emotional." "I'm one of the most emotional people here." Many of these listeners report that they cry when they are deeply moved. Indeed, one person asks the senior minister for a pre-sermon advisory as to the emotionality of the sermon. "If it's a four-tissue sermon, or a five-tissue sermon, I'm supposed to know ahead of time so I'm prepared."[8]

Moreover, a deeper understanding of pathos is characteristic of people who hear the sermon via this channel: Feeling is itself a mode of knowledge. It is awareness that is almost intuitive in nature and that cannot always be expressed in conventional language. Sometimes knowledge from the life of feeling can be expressed through artistic media (e.g., poetry, music, dance, short story, novel, film, sculpture, paintings). However, sometimes this knowledge can hardly be expressed.

Several people who hear the sermon through pathos settings speak of the relationship between feeling and knowledge in this deeper way. A listener points to this same phenomenon when speaking about trying to pray after the destruction of the World Trade Center in New York City on September 11, 2001.

I think our ministers are very powerful in their prayers in the service of worship, and I think that makes a difference, too, because during the week you sometimes feel like you just can't get it out. Just like this week, with what happened, you wanted to pray and ask God to help, but how did you ask for it? Sometimes they can hit on that, help you come up with the words.

The desire to pray was within this listener, but it took the spoken prayers of the pastor to name that otherwise formless, but powerful, desire. This incident points to one of the important functions that preachers can perform for people who hear the sermon through pathos perspectives: preachers can help them name their emotions so that the parishioners can better respond to those feelings.

A fuller example comes from a person commenting on the role of stories in sermons. As the comment begins, the interviewee offers a conventional understanding of how stories function in sermons ("You can hang the message on the story most of the time.") but then interprets feeling as a realm of trans-verbal awareness:

One of the great things about our pastor's sermons is that the pastor tells stories. You can hang the message on the story most of the time. As a matter of fact, one of the great sermons... A year ago, almost exactly, on the night of All Souls Day, our pastor preached. There was just an absolutely tremendous ecclesiastical service. Then there was this long reading of the necrology. But during the sermon the pastor talked about the living having communion with the dead. The pastor described how, when the pastor was at seminary up in [another state], they gathered on All Souls Day, and they marched in the chapel, and they marched out to the cemetery where they paid their respects to various members of the faculty, ministers who had preceded them there, and so forth. Then they read the necrology. I remember that sermon. It was a great sermon. Then they read the necrology. The music, the things that were done at the altar. It was a most moving type of experience.

Later in the interview, the respondent returns to that sermon when asked to cite a sermon that caused this person to feel differently.

A feeling, emotion...feel differently. I tell you this sermon on All Saints Day; I was moved to the point of tears. I think the whole experience was that I had a feeling of closeness, identity with people dead, my parents. My mother hadn't died yet. She died at the age of 100 and almost three months in March of this year. There's a boy I grew up with. We grew up in the same town. We went to the university together. We both went off to the army together. He was killed in France. I came back. It could have been me rather than him. [The interviewee cries]. I found an identity with him then that I simply hadn't felt before. It was the sermon in part. The sermon set the context. It gave the enveloping structure for the whole evening's liturgical experience. It was just a tremendous experience.

After commenting on the silence that followed that sermon and service, the interviewee mentions that "when the Protestants broke off from the Roman Catholic Church, they didn't want all these kneelings and crossings and incense and candles and stained glass and statues and all these other things…Everything was going to be intellectual." However, this listener reminds us:

Words are just incapable of expressing the complexities of religious faith. That's why you need all these impertinences. Most Protestant churches don't get it. Even in [the high liturgical church this person attends], which I know best, it's not always achieved. Confessions of faith, creeds, formularies–they're all important because if you don't have them, people can get up and say, "Well, what I mean by this. What I think is important is really important." You've got to be able to say, "That's not right. That's not what we believe. We believe this, and it says so in the [name of major creedal affirmation of faith used in the denomination], or whatever you've got, the call to confession and so forth. But once you've got that stuff, you don't have very much at all because it's impossible to express in human language the depths, the complexities, the mysteries of religious faith. You need to engage the whole person–the mind, the senses, the smell, the hearing, the eyes. You need to engage the whole person.

On the one hand, the use of words set the stage for this listener's moment of trans-verbal insight. On the other hand, too many words (especially "yakking" from the pulpit or even by parishioners in the pews) can get in the way of the deep knowledge that comes to expression in the life of feeling. There are moments when, "You don't talk." The message is in the silence.

From this listener's point of view, one of the things a preacher can do to help encourage the faithful who experience knowledge in this way is to use language carefully to shape moments that can engage the whole person and in which the knowledge of feeling can have some space in which to be absorbed, and, as possible, named. The preacher, however, needs to be careful not to "yuk it up" with too many words.

Another listener was not a church-goer, but then says, "I can't explain why. I just started coming." That was about twenty-five years ago, and this person has become quite active in the congregation. When asked to recall the effects of sermons, this person replies, "I can think of times when I was uplifted. I can think of times when I cried. I can think of times when I felt uncomfortable, times when I was inspired. But what it was that inspired me, I don't know." The feeling of inspiration was palpable, but "What the meat of the sermon was, I don't know." Given some time to reflect on what, in preaching, causes this person to feel uplifted or to feel uncomfortable, the listener avers:

> The ones that move me are ones that deal with extraordinary kindnesses and acts of selfless generosity. These usually end up being things that are in the stories or anecdotes the preacher will use in a sermon. I find that my spouse will be affected the same way, and we won't be the only ones. The preacher just has a way of winging these out. How the preacher does it, I don't know, but it does have that quality. I do feel it…and you make certain kinds of connections with things you can't distance yourself from. A couple of times, the sermons have done this, sort of link together something that is totally unrelated to the sermon. When John Kennedy was killed I was living in [another city]. I was in graduate school. I remember exactly where I was when I heard about it. I remember the weekend was terribly bleak. We were watching the funeral on television, and they started playing the Navy Hymn and I started to cry. Now I can't hear the Navy Hymn without crying. The kind of experiences like that the preacher will touch on. The preacher may not mean to touch on, but it just happens to be on where I'm making a connection that will affect me in some way. That doesn't happen in all contexts. It seems to me only in church does this kind of thing crop up.

This listener anticipates a motif to which we attend further attention below—namely that stories often stir people. But even more, this person opens a window on the fact that the life of feeling is often hidden from conscious awareness, is vast and powerful, and its parts are interconnected.

This subconscious network of emotions and associations explains, at least on occasion, why listeners sometimes react to sermons in ways that the preacher finds altogether surprising. The sermon has sparked a connection deep in the listener's self. Preachers seldom need to be discouraged by such seemingly random associations. Indeed, such occasions may be important experiences of trans-conscious awareness. Though neither parishioner nor pastor can fully name it, something profound goes on.

Why do such experiences "crop up" for our interviewee in church? "I think it's a place where I feel safe, where I can let that sort of thing happen without embarrassment. If it were any other context, I don't think I could." The service of worship is sanctuary. Ministers and other congregational leaders perform a significant service to members such as this one by helping the service of worship, and the broader life of the congregation, become an environment in which people feel free to express their emotions. Indeed, creating such a "safe space" is itself an enactment of the gospel for such folk.

Perspectives similar to these do occur in interviews with persons who listen on ethos and logos settings. However, they are more characteristic (and are often expressed with greater force) by folk who approach sermons through pathos.

Seeking Sermons That Inspire, Move, Stir

Congregants who listen to sermons through pathos settings share with listeners on the other settings hope that sermons will help them identify material in the Bible that they can learn and apply to their everyday worlds. They often explicitly add the hope that sermons will affect them emotionally. For instance, a listener describes a good preacher whom this listener heard for many years.

> This preacher's strengths are not only that the sermons are biblically based, the preacher is very talented in the way the preacher can illustrate with words. The preacher has the ability to paint pictures and use appropriate transitions into life application. The preacher is a very strong speaker and is very talented at putting a lot of information and emotion and strength into a sermon.

This listener amplifies the role of emotion in receiving the sermon.

> I hope to feel closer to God at that point [i.e. hearing a sermon]. We're in God's house and hopefully we've prepared ourselves at that point to listen. I want to be drawn as much as possible. Sometimes it's more and sometimes it's less, and sometimes I think we have something that every person—you just feel like you're getting deeper, and that's what I hope that people are preparing themselves for and experiencing.

Not surprisingly, this listener says elsewhere, "Sometimes, authority is a feeling. Sometimes it's an emotion."

People who hear the sermon through pathos often use language such as "inspire," "lift up," "fill," "stir," or "move" to describe what they hope will happen when they hear a sermon, as we hear when an African American parishioner is asked why people come for preaching. "Because it's emotional. You get emotional. A lot of people get emotional. They say 'Amen.' They wouldn't even know where to be saved except for preaching. Preaching is emotional. It strikes people's emotions. They react toward it." The interviewer inquires what, about preaching, touches emotions. "Each person looks at it differently, but I think with preaching, they feel it right then. A person just fills up right then, and at that moment they forget about other things in their life. So I think right then it strikes them emotionally." People come to church because "you know that you can come to be filled." The desire to be filled is the reason not just for listening to the sermon but for coming to worship. Being filled does not depend upon the sermon alone. "A lot of times, not the sermon, maybe the music, but it will be something. It's emotional. I just feel like you've just got to shout something. Some, they say, 'Amen.'"

Another listener shows quite vividly that some listeners on the pathos wavelength think that emotion in the sermon is not an end in itself but leads to thought and action. A sermon "begins to stir within me particular emotions that challenge you. Are you really walking the walk?" The parishioner goes on:

> What preaching does particularly—I like it in the African American context—is to charge the air with words from God. Scripture says, "How can you hear the word unless it's preached?" So I look at our preachers as being an instrument used by God to challenge God's people to move into action. To create in them such a love of God's creation...and humankind, that we are always challenged to do a little more, come a little bit closer, move a little bit out, come in. Whatever way the Spirit moves, I think it does that. I am not one of those individuals that feel there's that one instant. Sometimes in the preaching moment I am moved to tears. Sometimes I'm challenged or convicted, and sometimes it takes a couple of weeks or maybe months to sit up there and say that's what they were talking about. The preacher was trying to move me.

This listener calls attention to the fact that emotions and their effects are not simply ephemeral. It may take a long time to process the knowledge of feeling generated by the sermon, and the effects can be far-reaching.

Qualities That Evoke Pathos in Sermons

Many of the interviewees seem to be quite conscious of qualities in sermons that evoke pathos. Often the listeners alert us to these characteristics in response to questions about what, in sermons, engages them, as well as in response to questions that invited them to talk about sermons that stirred their emotions. The telling of stories, listeners in the pathos quadrant say, is the most frequently cited trait in preaching that moves them. In fact, almost every one of the interviewees in this group makes that observation. Some listeners are also moved by other kinds of material.

For these folk, stories often function at multiple levels. They hear some stories illustrating the main point(s) of the sermon—as a listener quoted just above said, a story is a hook on which the preacher can hang the message of the sermon. We hear this perspective from one of the people in the study, a teacher, who spontaneously gives a bit of a lecture from the person's classroom.

> I use an example when talking to students about the whole storytelling enterprise. If you're driving along the interstate, and you're stopped by the police and given a ticket for speeding, when you get back to the dorm, you tell people what happened to you. What you're trying to do is to get people to be sympathetic to you, not to the police officer, that you have been done an injustice. Your whole purpose in telling the story is to persuade people of this, or to tell somebody, to relay to somebody how you felt about it. It's all emotion.

Preachers, according to this listener, should adopt this perspective on their use of stories: "I have to persuade you that what I'm saying is legitimate, an authentic way to interpret what we've read from the Bible this morning. This is the way I understand it, and I'm going to try to get you to understand it the same way I do." Stories play a role because, "Whatever's happened to you, you want to tell somebody else, and you want them to be sympathetic." The goal–persuasion–depends upon pathos (developing sympathy).

The experience of hearing the story, for these folk, is a part of the meaning of the story, as are the emotions that are invoked by it. Stories from the preacher's own life are important for some of these listeners (as for persons who enter the sermon through ethos channels). In the midst of ruminating on some good preachers who were storytellers, one listener recalls a well known preacher:

> I find there is an element that I think is true we haven't mentioned. This is extremely true with a well-known preacher and I think it's true for all great preachers. There's a confessional aspect about their preaching. This well-known preacher uses the preacher's own self more than anyone else as an illustration. This is a confessional type of preaching and I think it is very effective, because what it does is that they are not better than you. They are the same as you are. They have lost some. They have won some. They are out there. I think this touches people.

Although this listener does include ethos elements in the description of confessional preaching (e.g. "they are the same as you are"), the ethos qualities are clearly in the service of pathos: "This touches people." A preacher can call forth passion in people by telling "how an event, a person, a story around that person changed the preacher's life."

Some preachers tell stories that are about people in the congregation or known by people in the congregation.

Our minister will tell us anecdotes and he generally says, "This is about someone at another church. It's not about someone here." Sometimes the pastor will say, "This is about someone right here, and they know I'm going to tell you this." So you know it's not speaking out of turn. That immediately makes it very relevant. This is one of our own who has gone through whatever it is.

This listener puts forward that a key to the success of the use of such stories is to secure permission from the persons from the congregation who are involved in the story and to communicate that permission to the congregation.[9]

Taking further the notion of knowledge being communicated through feeling, a listener with an education background says, "I come from a theory of different ways of knowing and different ways of learning and realize that people receive messages in different ways." Effective preachers utilize "at least two or three of those tactics." This perspective comes to light when commenting on "effective preachers."

I have witnessed movement as a way of effectively communicating a message, be it a sermon that's done through liturgical dance or a sermon that is simply a pastor so in the moment and so moved by what he or she is saying that the repetition of the gesture or the particular phrase. It may be completely automatic and unplanned, but the fact that it's always recurring when they say something really powerful. Or someone who's drawn to either a visual presentation or to a movement, a kinesthetic kind of learning can really connect with them at that moment.

A specific instance of body movement with a trans-verbal quality is described:

I think there was a very effective sermon that was done here a couple of years ago with liturgical dance—spoken word and liturgical dance—and I felt people were equally impacted throughout the sanctuary that day. I've found that while the sermon...might not have been as effective in word, the Holy Spirit was definitely present and you could feel the energy, and people were equally rallied around that sermon, and that message subsequently impacted the congregation.

This person who witnessed the event does not, probably cannot, say in straightforward language what the impact and meaning of the sermon were. It is clear, however, that the sermon communicated on the level of feeling through the kinesthetic mode of the sermon.

Several people from different congregations in the pathos listening cohort indicate that they like it when the preacher does not make the point of the sermon explicit. They like to be left to ponder the implications of the sermon for themselves. A person in the interview groups summarizes the effect of such an approach:

> To summarize into one sentence, they make you want to be better. Now, you've got to figure it out because the preachers have not given you step-by-step directions. How do I do that? They haven't told you how to do that. They've left it open for you, but the content of what they have said, what they have illustrated for you, is a better life, a better way of living, a better way for doing things, more passion.

The listener appreciates getting the direction of the sermon (to help people live in better ways) but also appreciates having the freedom to sort out how to apply the main idea of the sermon to the context of the listener's own life.

One obvious implication is that preachers need to include stories in sermons. The implied qualification in some of the above remarks is that stories in sermons should reflect the character of real life, that is, should be fraught with the same kinds of questions, tensions, hopes, difficulties and ambiguities that are a part of life in the everyday world. The listeners interviewed in this study are not likely to be moved by stories that seem too good to be true or that oversimplify life. Sermons can include stories from the preacher's own life, providing such stories do not appear so frequently that people begin to react, "Oh, no, not another one from the preacher's own life."[10]

Emotional Discomfort as Occasion for Becoming More Faithful

Listeners on pathos settings often feel uncomfortable in response to some sermons when preachers say or do things that are simply distracting. These feelings get in the way of more positive feelings as well as ideas that might be important to the listener. For instance, one of the interviewees tells of going to the funeral of a parent at which the minister did not know the decedent. "The sermon was totally unrelated to my parent and the family...The thing from this preacher was so disturbing that when we had to go back several years later for the other parent's funeral, it was a different pastor, not that one again. We refused to have anything to do with the first pastor."

However, many of these listeners call attention to another kind of discomfort—an uneasiness created by the sermon that prompts growth. Preachers help listeners focus on difficult circumstances. In these cases, considering the discomfiture becomes an occasion for identifying things that people need to do to become more faithful. These considerations help listeners focus on ways that are constructive (even if immediately painful).

The most vivid expression for this phenomenon articulated by one of the interviewees, whom we mentioned briefly in chapter 1, is a "squirmer," that is, a message that causes people to squirm.

> The squirmy ones where, I guess, we all have things we say and do without stopping to think about them. Those are the ones that point out usually how blessed we are, and yet, at the same time, how selfish for not sharing more of what we've got. Then you feel, "The preacher is talking about me, and is right. I could be more generous. I could be more giving. I do have more than I need." Or on those occasions about ways I behave, how we treat street people, how we deal with people who for some reason have a grudge against us or the people we have a grudge against. Occasionally there'll be a forgiveness sermon that the preacher throws in there…Usually you can find something in those sermons that speaks to a failure that you recognize that you don't talk about. You don't want to admit, but you know it's there, and it's hidden, but God knows about it. You think, "Well, I should do something," but whether or not I do anything, I remember that I am guilty. I've committed a fault. I've committed a sin, not necessarily a sin, but I've done something I shouldn't have done. I should be doing something to make up for that.

This listener interprets squirmers in an explicitly theological framework. The question is, "What do you think God is doing during the time of homily?"

> Hmm. God may be one of those Olympic judges who hold up the cards with the ratings numbers [chuckle]. God's maybe saying, "Where did the preacher get a crazy idea like that?" I think basically what God is doing is God is between us in the sermon. I think it's God that makes us squirm. God is the one that touches us rather than…It's the words, yes, but it's…I guess the Holy Spirit's in the language and in the sermon itself, and that's what we're reacting to. It's not just the words. It's an emotional reaction.

We return to the theme of the relationship between the Spirit and emotions in the next part of the chapter. For now, it is enough to note that this listener believes that God through Spirit is at work in the emotional response described as "squirming."

When reflecting on the most important things that happen in the congregation, one person gives a strong evaluation of creative discomfort:

> The most important things that happen in this congregation. I think that this congregation is challenging in that I don't think it allows anyone to be particularly comfortable with anything other than

the fact that they are welcome here, and that they will be included. I find so many things in worship and in this congregational life that are challenging and that push me just a little bit further beyond my comfort zone than I would probably do on my own.

This congregant thinks that this attitude is constituent of the congregation itself. "I would guess that most of my comrade parishioners, while they may not articulate it that way, have a similar sense that they are pushed."

When developing a sermon (or part of a sermon) with persons in mind who listen on pathos settings, the preacher can think about including material that may make such persons uncomfortable when the uneasiness is the kind that should prompt the type of self-inventory depicted by the listeners in this study. As possible, a preacher should avoid material that is simply distracting. Of course, given the complicated nature of the life of feeling, the sermon could spark a reaction that is altogether unintended and unanticipated, in which case, the preacher can make appropriate pastoral responses and hope that all involved will respond to the presence of the Holy Spirit that is "between us," as a listener above said.

God Moves through Feeling

Several persons who participate in the sermon through logos settings speak extensively about their perception that God moves through feeling. Several speak more specifically of the Holy Spirit stirring them through this venue.[11] We have already observed this phenomenon in listeners cited above.

We hear similar perceptions that God stirs people through the life of feeling in other listeners, such as the one who says:

I can feel God there at the time of preaching. I wish I could think of a Sunday in particular, because that doesn't happen all the time, but I know God is with us all the time. I can't think of any specific instances but that the feeling does happen frequently. There are times when you can feel the vibration in the people. You can feel it.

For this listener, the experience of the Spirit through feeling is visceral: "You can feel the vibration in the people."

Another listener believes that the Holy Spirit works at the time of the sermon through the life of feeling.

Also when the Holy Spirit is at work in a congregation while the preacher is preaching, that's also a work of the Holy Spirit in my own heart or in your heart that would not occur anywhere else…Two things. Number one, the pastor is to be a prophet in terms of giving us the word of God on an issue. That's number one. Number two is if the Holy Spirit is in the message, and in the congregation, then I know in my life that the Holy Spirit can speak to me, and I can get insights and emotions, if that's a good word, that I would not have gotten anywhere else through the sermon.

The Spirit works not only through feeling, but also through the word. Another person also believes that God speaks in both the "written word, the logos [yes, the interviewee used the word 'logos'], and that which quickens the heart, that divine influence upon the heart that exemplifies itself in a person's life."

> I guess I tell that a sermon has authority by the Spirit, and that may come in different forms. It may be loud. It may be very still. A lot of it depends upon what the Lord is quickening in me. That's why I say I guess I would know by the Spirit. Sometimes it may be challenging if it's something I say. "Ooh, ouch, ooh. I hear you, Lord." It may just be a remark that I hear that someone is saying. Quite often I have Trinity Broadcasting Network at home while I'm getting dressed to go to work, while I'm getting dressed to come to church, and later in the evening...and a word will come forth and I'll say, "Ooh. Oh, I hear you Lord." There are a lot of real penetrating things that come to me just in little sentences here and there...

For this listener, pathos and logos interplay. The quickening (pathos) results in a feeling ("Ooh, ouch") that is accompanied by a recognition of a message ("I hear you, Lord"). A statement that this person hears may be confirmed by the feeling of being quickened.

A few listeners address an important theological issue: How does one distinguish a feeling that is a lure from the Spirit from a feeling that is not? One says:

> I try to listen to a sermon candidly and openly. As I say, when I come in to the service of worship, I come to hear a word of God. I'm able to determine whether or not it is a word of God, not almost instantly–I can't say that. But I have been moved by the Spirit and I can hear within my spirit the truth that lies in the sermon. I'm also able to verify what's in that sermon by the scripture itself. So it's a whole process that comes.
>
> I believe God is a God of love, not of hate. Therefore, those passages and those scriptures and sermons that speak in that language resonate in my spirit. I believe God is a God of justice. I believe God is a deliverer. So when sermons are crafted to speak in terms of deliverance of people, I believe that is a word from God. Then I believe God recognizes diversity as well as the unity of the body.

So, then, as I listen to a sermon, I listen for the elements of my upbringing—those things that I've seen in the scripture that to me reflect Jesus. That tells me this is word-inspired. This is God-inspired. It's an inner feeling. It's an inner feeling, but one that I think has to be confirmed with the word of God. For example, if you were going to pick up a gun and shoot everybody that you see on the street of a different race, that's pure evil. It does not confirm the word of God.

This listener puts criteria on the table by which to gauge when emotions are the work of the Spirit: when they promote love and justice, when they speak of deliverance and support diversity, and when they are confirmed by the word of God (which, for this listener, is the Bible). Elsewhere in the interview, this member of the study group acknowledges that the Bible itself must be interpreted. The latter criterion, then, is more complicated than may appear at first.

If the preacher agrees theologically with these listeners that the Spirit does move through the life of feeling, the preacher can help them determine the criteria by which to distinguish feelings that (likely) emanate from the Spirit and those that do not.[12] The preacher can also help such folk try to name, as much as possible, the ways that they are moved both so they can be more clear about what the Spirit says to them through feeling and so the insights that come to them through feeling can become a part of wider conversation in the congregation.

Feeling in Embodiment Encourages Emotion

As we observed in chapter 1, interviewees from all three settings share most perceptions of embodiment, and where differences occur, the diversity can seldom be correlated with specific people who listen on particular settings. One difference that is associated with a particular setting is with pathos. Many people in this listening group speak with force and detail about the importance of embodiment reflecting and encouraging feeling. For example, a listener says:

I want to feel that the minister is engaged. I don't want to feel like we're listening to a book being read. I want to have the sense that this is meaningful to them, too. It's not just for our benefit, but this is coming through them. Sometimes that's by eye contact, by the volume or depth of the voice. Sometimes it's by coming out from behind the pulpit and moving in different ways. Sometimes it's by being more animated or more meaningful as opposed to "Here it is and we're just going to go through it." I think that sense that it's coming through them as messenger and that they are affected as well, I think that's what engages the congregation.

As this listener reveals in the body of the interview, to be "meaningful" is to have a significant emotional component, to be "affected."

A listener who has previously stressed that the Holy Spirit moves through preacher and congregation in an emotional way says that the major quality in the sermon's embodiment is

> just the overall expression so that I can tell this is heartfelt. This is compassion. If the preacher was to stand up in the pulpit and tell me this is how I should walk the Christian walk and it came across—I'm talking about the delivery here—it came across with no compassion, no emphasis. Like if I would just "This is how you should walk the Christian way dadadadadada" and I had no emotion. I just stood there and said it to you. It would take away from my feeling. I feel with my heart first of all, but I am also moved by the expression of a pastor in delivering the word, "God said…" The hand gestures bring the word. The word alone will bring to me, but it's the hand gestures that I can actually see and feel more intense about.

This listener wants to feel compassionate energy in the preacher's voice. The listener likes energy and excitement, but expressed in a tone of voice that communicates compassion, that is, that the preacher cares about the congregation and the message.

Embodiment with emotion is not associated with one particular style, but can take place through a variety of modes.

> I don't believe in theatrical performances in the pulpit. I believe that there are charismatic people in this world, and you can use those to grab attention, but those types of things don't normally grab me. I look at them for what they are. But within our tradition, the hum if you will, there is a group of African American preachers that still have a hum or almost a singing motion as they begin preaching. Then there are those ministers like Howard Thurman who just speaks—his presence, his feelings. There are some that I know that can just bring you to tears with just good thematical development. The tone in which they speak, almost with an air of authority that is uncommon, but yet a humbling of the spirit all alone, trying to resonate a point.

From this slant, embodiment that communicates feeling is not a particular style but a quality with which the feeling in the listener resonates.

Of course, preachers should embody sermons with eye contact, use of the voice, energy, movement, and presence. In addition, to connect with persons who hear the sermon on pathos channels, preachers should speak with emotion that is appropriate to them as persons, to the content of the message, and to the congregational setting.

Pathos Settings Interact with Ethos

As we have repeatedly noticed in connection with other settings, a person who takes in the sermon through a particular setting typically processes the preacher's appeals from the other settings through the listener's particular one. Most of the parishioners who listen to the sermon through pathos settings perceive the character of the preacher in ways that are consistent with the picture of ethos in traditional rhetoric. For example, these listeners honor the call or anointment of the preacher, and the integrity and education. One listener likes to "have a feeling that preaching is not just a job." Another interviewee describes a particular pastor who is also a good preacher.

> I think it's from the heart, and strictly from the Spirit that moves that preacher. The preacher is really educated and really knows the scriptures. That preacher is definitely, I don't believe, a false prophet. That preacher tells it is like it is, and you're not going to heaven if…That preacher is a good person to believe in.

To this congregant, the preacher's sermons sound as if they come from the heart, and as if the Spirit is moving. These particularly pathos qualities combine with the listener's belief that the preacher is educated, a true prophet, and straightforward, to convince this person that the preacher is trustworthy (traditional ethos virtues).

Many pathos-inclined listeners respond to their perception of the preacher's character (and other ethos matters) from the standpoint of how that perception makes them feel. They tend to be favorably disposed towards a preacher with whom they perceive positive relational feelings, and negatively disposed towards preachers with whom they have feelings of disappointment.

Not surprisingly, people who hear the sermon on pathos settings perceive relationships through the experience of feeling. These folk often describe relationships from the perspective of feeling. Even more, relationships are a source of feeling for some listeners on ethos settings. These tendencies are true when persons in the pathos cohort speak of relationships with the pastor, with God, with other people in the community, and with persons and communities in the larger world.

One of the most important ways that these listeners develop a positive impression of the preacher is through experiences with that person both inside the sermon and in everyday life that result in positive feelings, as the following incident exemplifies:

> Our pastor is so sensitive to other people and their needs. The day after my father died, I was reading [leading a part of a mid-week service in the congregation]. It was a Thursday noon. When I got to the necrology and read my father's name, I started to cry. The

pastor just reached out with a purificator and put it in my hand. The pastor didn't anticipate this. Did not look at me. Didn't do anything. The pastor just reached out. In the same way that when there's an ambulance going by and we're at the altar, just without stopping what the pastor is doing, makes the sign of the cross. It's something that's become so instinctive and so natural. The pastor just has that sensitivity to how other people are feeling. We're hoping this pastor stays here a long time.

When the preacher steps into the pulpit, this listener responds emotionally.

Another listener makes a similar observation, but with a more communal point of view, when remembering a former preacher who

> had a very strong presence in the pulpit, really committed to social justice issues. What else I remember about this former minister is that the minister knew the congregation. This minister knew that the people the minister pastored and would preach to that. This minister would address, of course, not individuals but things that were happening to us corporately, and was willing to learn. This minister was really humble about what the minister knew and would often say in the pulpit, "This week I learned from somebody I was talking to." So this minister really had an emotional connection with the congregation. This minister really loved the congregation.

In a subsequent response, the hearer expands the sense of emotional connection to even broader corporate life:

> There's also that emotional connection with connecting the congregation with issues or with the world and seeing both of those in the light of faith and what we can do about that. How does that affect us daily? I know that during some real crisis of this church— we had quite a bit of money embezzled by our administrative assistant at one time—the preaching was very kind and nurturing. I respect this congregation immensely in the way they handled those kinds of situations. I think that one of the minister's preachings really helped to cement that and to say, "Yes, there's been a loss. We need to grieve our losses. We need to be gentle and kind and understanding, and we need to stand our ground." I think this minister helped to guide and lead us through sermons as well as congregational meetings and those kinds of things.

The feeling of positive emotional relationship with the preacher is very important for many listeners in this cohort to engage the sermon as fully as they can.

Still another listener comments on how the preacher's display of emotion becomes a point by which the listener identifies with the preacher as well as a source of authority for this hearer. "A sermon has authority, in a very human way has authority, when it has touched a point or hit on a point that I know deep down to be true, but that I often, for whatever reason, don't want to admit." This person tells a dramatic story about a sermon that caused this person to think and act differently:

> I was worshiping at a congregation in another city and I found the pastor to be an incredibly effective preacher and an incredibly effective speaker and very emotional. The first time I saw that preacher cry in the pulpit, I was incredibly, incredibly moved that the preacher revealed such vulnerability to the hundreds of people that were sitting in that house of worship. Seeing the passion and...the preacher is sort of a hippie's crusader for peace and justice and human rights.
>
> I had up to that point sort of emotionally resigned from the [name of denomination] Church and said, "The church is in a mess. It's got to get itself together before I want to be part of it again." Part of the word that was revealed to me that day was the fact that you've gone around and visited different denominations and different places of worship and not become a member, just sort of stayed on the periphery waiting for the [name of denomination] Church to smarten up. Once they get straightened out, then you'll go. I had this call about why not be a part of the solution; I was like, "Whoa!" So now I can't wait for them to change, but I can go, join, and I have to take a role in helping to change or help it emerge, help it grow, help it evolve.
>
> While I can't tell you exactly what was being said in the pulpit at that moment, that experience definitely changed my course because I became a member of a church that really impacted me. That ended up bringing me to this church [name of the present congregation], because I didn't want to come back here when I moved back to town, but I had been a member here at a much earlier time. They said they stood for something, and that I should at least go visit them. I saw how it had evolved and changed. I came regularly. All of a sudden I heard this call to be a [name of a particular kind of leader in the congregation]. It just sort of kept building and building.

For this listener, the preacher's public release of emotion helped create a setting in which the listener's life of feeling made associations that empowered the listener to make an important decision to return to church. The sermon on the Sunday this person was installed into the leadership position was "quite moving." While describing this event, the listener provides further insight into how feeling functions as mode of knowledge.

> Emotionally, I was pretty heightened that day. Basically a sermon about hearing the call of God and the gifts that all people in the church bring, I think, was a pretty impressive message for me...A year later, when they installed the next class of leaders, our pastor preached that sermon as well. It was about hearing the call of God and heeding the call of God. I remember starting to cry in that sermon the same way I had the year before, because it was just a powerful message to say I don't necessarily always know why I feel compelled to do this or agree to do this, but I did feel called.

This auditor "doesn't necessarily know why" the auditor "feels compelled" to accept the call, but the sense of its rightness is unmistakable. Sermons have created space within which the listener's emotional knowledge can be released, and the listener makes significant life decisions in response.

Some of the people in this group point to the pastor faithfully performing ministerial duties as reason to pay attention to the sermon. Often such remarks are related to feeling, as in the case of the following:

> To be approachable is a good trait for a pastor. I think it's good for them to mingle with everybody after worship and talk, to be accessible after church. Sometimes just coming out of church and having just heard it, I know it's hard because they have a schedule. But they always offer that if you need to talk after church, "Please come and talk to us, because at that moment, those emotions and that problem may be..." So, to be accessible.

The person making this statement frequently cries during worship. The opportunity to talk with the pastors about the feelings generated by the sermon is important; this listener trusts the pastors with those feelings. Such pastoral availability also encourages this person to feel free to respond similarly in subsequent services of worship.

For some listeners, gender, feeling, and relationship function in an intertwined pathos way. A woman interviewee remembers a woman pastor in another congregation.

> Well, I should say there was a woman at another congregation where I was previously a member that I really appreciated her sermons. Her sermons were much more feminine. They were more emotional. Yet they were from the wisdom of a woman. They were very wise and insightful, very insightful. The emotion was there with her. She was a touching...she could touch your heart. I always looked forward to when she was doing the sermon because I knew she would catch my attention. She was a good storyteller.

The pastor and the parishioner had a good relationship. "Maybe that's why I felt like she could touch me on stage, because I knew her personally." The personal bond helped create a space within which this listener felt free to experience powerful emotions.

When developing a sermon (or part of a sermon) with the people who hear sermons through pathos settings in mind, a preacher needs to consider how the congregation's feelings about the preacher can enhance, or frustrate, the message. In the case of the former, the preacher can help listeners transfer the positive qualities of their perception of the preacher to the message, and take advantage of that feeling of trust to stretch and challenge the congregation. In the event of the latter, the preacher needs to consider what sort of material, in the sermon itself, might give such listeners an impetus to change their perception. Of course, in wider parish life, the preacher needs to try to speak and act in ways that encourage positive feelings (insofar as the preacher can do so while maintaining personal and theological integrity).

The person who takes in the sermon through pathos settings is likely to be energized when the preacher calls attention to the feelings that are a part of the relationships in the sermon. In the sermon, the preacher might comment on relationships of materials that are included in the sermon. For example, insofar as one can tell on the basis of critical exegesis, what roles do feelings play among the setting, actions, and characters within the world of a biblical text? The pastor could help the congregation name and reflect on the feelings generated as the congregation responds to the text. A preacher might tell the major stories in the sermon from the standpoint of the feeling dynamics that are intimated in the stories themselves and in the listeners' responses to those stories. Of course, the preacher should pursue such questions in an open way—not prescribing how people should (or necessarily do) feel, but leaving room for them to feel.

Pathos Settings Interact with Logos

Some of the leading motifs in how persons who listen to sermons on pathos settings interact with the content of the sermon are similar to those of persons who enter sermons through logos settings. However, quite a few congregants who attend to sermons through logos settings tend to regard pathos as a secondary mode of experience, and even that should be distrusted. For people who listen to the sermon on pathos settings, however, feeling is a not an accessory but a fundamental mode of knowledge. They look to logos to help them understand feeling. Receiving a clear idea is not enough; many people who listen on pathos settings do not feel that meaning is truly achieved until something stirs within. Even when these listeners cannot fully name the significance of the inner life, they are often willing to live with a certain measure of ambiguity.

Feelings Alert Listeners to Thoughts

The occurrence of emotion in a listener who approaches the sermon through pathos settings can be the occasion for thought. The person who enters the sermon through pathos settings often experiences such emotion as a signal that they need to pay attention to an idea or relationship. Sometimes the thought focuses on the emotion itself, such as, "Why am I feeling distant from this preacher?" (see below). But more often, the presence of emotion in connection with an idea sparks reflection on the idea itself.

A listener indicates the central role of pathos in sparking reflection, and even change, in describing what this person hopes will happen as a result of listening to the sermon. "Again I keep going back to the emotional hook [that sermons need to have for this listener] because that's what really drives me to change–something said about something that's mentioned in the sermon or if there's some intellectual-emotional connection that I haven't made before."

The same listener recalls an occasion when an emotional sermon became "a pivotal force" in theological thinking.

> There was one Thanksgiving sermon that a friend of mine gave. This preacher was talking about reading a newspaper article about a man who had beaten his wife and then murdered her and shot himself. The newspaper article said the children were not injured even though the children were in the house. The preacher went on to ask, "What is injury? How can they say these children are not injured?"
>
> That sermon for me was a pivotal force in thinking about Jesus and the presence of Jesus in my faith and giving me much gentler ways of thinking about my faith and the way I approach myself and who Jesus was, rather than God being this harsh judge of character and "You're always in this box or that box." The preacher talked about Jesus suffering the way the children did in a way. The abused woman had suffered. I think that sermon for me was pivotal in I guess maybe deciding to remain Christian and being able to live with Christianity as a faith of love rather than of judgment.

The interviewer says quietly, "Just that simple story."

> Yes. And then connecting Jesus with the suffering woman. You hear those words over and over again, but it just seems to me that at some point a sermon or something else will touch you on a level that you've never been touched before by something else. Something you think you've known all your life, you now say, "Oh! That's right!" You have this profound insight that somebody helped you reach.

The telling of the story of the household tragedy, and raising the question about injury, is an "emotional hook" for this listener. The decision to remain a Christian is also motivated by pathos—the connection between Jesus and the suffering woman. For this listener, the experience of pathos is the occasion for significant reflection, and the pathos itself is part of the content of the reflection.

At the same time it is important to realize that for many listeners who come into the sermon on pathos settings, significant ideas stir emotion.

> The preacher is bringing us the word of God. That's the overall thing—teaching, explicating, clarifying. Even if it's not an emotional idea, you get emotional just because of the content. I can tell when the preacher is visibly shaken, although the preacher is not trying to cry or any of those superficial things. Just the preacher's demeanor will change, and the delivery will change. That impacts me. It impacts my spouse, too, because I can feel it next to me.

The presence of emotion is not enough, by itself, to certify the validity or the importance of an idea, but, for this listener, the presence of emotion in the preacher and in the listener prompts this congregant to be alert to the possibility that a significant idea is present.

Such listeners are most open to logos, content, when their feelings are stirred. Preachers can not only include material (such as stories) in the sermon that typically moves people, but can try to create an emotional fabric in the sermon in which to set ideas, and, as possible, include feeling elements in discussing those ideas. To be sure, a preacher cannot guarantee that a particular element in a sermon will call forth an emotional response, but some sermons will remain emotionally distant unless the preacher intentionally focuses on the importance of such material.

Sermons Interpret Feelings

Many people who listen to sermons through pathos settings are engaged when the preacher offers a theological interpretation of emotion that helps them name what is happening within them (and in the emotional dynamics of their relationships with other people). Several persons who approach preaching through pathos channels seek pastoral guidance in how to respond to emotions.

The following citation represents several in which congregants indicate that they are grateful for theological guidance in interpreting feeling and in responding to it:

> I know something that really helped me was a sermon one of our pastors gave about how, when people do things that hurt me, they do not hurt me purposefully. Usually it's to help themselves. That really hit home for me. I had gone through a divorce and had always wondered why my former spouse had done that to me.

Why? And when our minister said that and talked about…I can't tell you the verses that the pastor used right now. I just remember that it was such a meaningful sermon to me…Our minister helped me release that anger, that hurt, that it wasn't all my fault, that my former spouse didn't hate me, dislike me that much…That really did help me.

Practical consequences came from this sermon. "Now, it's just not so hurtful all the time. It did help me get rid of that anger and help me to be able to have the confidence when I needed to call for the kids or do something, I could call without dreading it."

Another listener contributes a similar example, though one that takes place in a communal setting. The community in which the congregation is located had suffered a dramatic tragedy on Saturday. The next day, the pastor did not preach the sermon that had been prepared before the tragedy but shifted the focus of the time allotted to the sermon as described in the following:

Instead of doing the sermon that day, since everybody seemed distraught and upset, the preacher just kind of laid down the sermon the preacher had for the day and talked with people, asked how they felt, and people raised their hands. Different people had different stories and different comments. I thought that was really interesting, because like I said sometimes without the sermon, what would church be? But then there are times like that when people really need to be together with the people they love and needing to express themselves. It makes you feel better. I think that is important.

The pastor's analysis of the congregation's orientation on that occasion draws an approval from this listener and also serves as a model for pastors in similar situations.

I think the members of the congregation were there because they're there every Sunday, but a lot of people wanted to be comforted. When you think of comfort, there is where I think of. In just regular life but also in times of tragedy, you kind of want to run to the church. The pastor had the ability to see that everybody was so upset that they probably weren't able to hear what he or she was saying anyway. I think they came away with quite a bit from that. The pastor had a little end thing that helped us.

The listener calls further attention to the role of pathos and interpretation in the situation.

I thought everybody got a lot out of the sermon-discussion about the tragedy, and everybody felt a little bit better because they did get to discuss it. You know you're not alone, and you got to share it with your church family...Everybody was talking about it before church, and then you could just feel it in the air. You feel that tension. Not that the discussion-sermon solved the problem, but I think it really helped everybody just to kind of get it out.

Here again we see the ability of the person who receives the sermon on pathos settings to live with a certain amount of ambiguity around unresolved emotional matters. However, note as well, the important role that pastoral leadership played in helping the community reach that point. The sermon time became a forum within which people could express their emotions.

The preacher is called to help people who listen to sermons on pathos channels make sense of their feelings, not only with respect to their own interior lives, but also to offer pastoral guidance in responding to those feelings. The sermon, of course, is not an appropriate setting for pastoral counseling.[13]

Being Touched Helps Listeners Remember

One of the most pervasive motifs in the interviews is the inability of interviewees to remember specific sermons, even when asked to recollect memorable sermons. A person typically remembers specific sermons when they were connected to important moments in that person's life. However, several listeners who hear the sermon via pathos settings say they remember sermons that touch them. A close examination of the interviews reveals that these listeners do not, in fact, recall the *content* of significantly more sermons than do persons who hear sermons via ethos and logos channels. People whose primary settings are pathos remember the feeling of being stirred.

A listener who, as a young adult, has returned to live in the parent's home, reports the effects of an emotionally moving sermon.

I know after I go to a really good church service, where the sermon just really touched me, I go home and talk about it with my mom. It sticks with me. All during the week, I'll be like, "Oh, you know what? I heard a sermon on that last weekend." I had somebody tell me the other day, "Boy, she knows what she's talking about." Not really. I've got a long ways to go.

A stirring sermon is not only emotionally satisfying for this listener, but empowers mission and strengthens the person's capacity to think and talk about matters that are important to Christian faith and life.

Another listener, when asked to recall a specific sermon, says, "You only know you feel good, and sometimes you don't know why you feel good. Or you go 'Ooooh' and you don't know exactly within yourself why that touched that chord to make you all of a sudden go 'Ooooh. Maybe I need to reevaluate.'" The interviewer prompts, "You remember the feeling, not necessarily the words that were said?"

> Yes. I have actually gotten a couple of the sermons by the pastors on tape, because they tape every service. I haven't actually, like, listened to them over and over again, but I've played bits and pieces of it to say, "How come I have this tape?" I put it in and go, "Oh, okay. It's because somehow the rhythm, the wording, the energy, the dynamics of the whole thing came together to make it an awesome moment for the congregation." It may not be specific wording. It's all those parts that create the message and the reaction and intensity to it.

Although the specific content may not come to mind after the service, the effect of the sermon lingers with this listener in the life of feeling.

Although the listeners in this group may not be able to remember the content of particular sermons, the emotional effects of sermons become a part of their reservoir of experience. For example, the awe of the "awesome moments" (to which reference was made above) becomes a part of the way in which the listener moves through life even when the conscious memory of the sermon, and even of the feeling, fades. This finding should be a source of great encouragement to preachers. Sermons continue to speak, through the life of feeling, long after voice and conscious memory have grown silent.

Although the attributes discussed in this chapter are rightly associated with people who listen on pathos settings, some of these characteristics also appear (in lesser frequency and intensity) among people who enter the sermon through ethos and logos settings. It should be noted that these attributes vary in degree from one person who listens on pathos settings to another. In any, the awareness that a significant number of members in the typical congregation hears the sermon on pathos settings should encourage the preacher to ask of every sermon, "Am I including material to help engage listeners who hear the sermon through pathos settings?"

CHAPTER 5

Three Settings and One Sermon

The Introduction to this book contains brief descriptions of three people in the same congregation who hear the sermon on different settings—Ethel through ethos settings, Lorenzo through logos settings, and Pat through pathos settings. What can a preacher do in a single sermon, or across a season of preaching, to have a good opportunity to communicate in a significant way with all three of these listeners and with the myriad of other combinations of settings that are found in people in the typical congregation? Even more important than communicating in a significant way with a community in whom people manifest diverse listening settings is developing appeals in sermons that are consistent with the deepest theological convictions of the preacher and the historic Christian tradition to which preacher and congregation belong.

This chapter first cautions preachers against using the findings in this volume simply to "give the people what they want." Implicit in the vocation of the preacher is measuring all attempts to communicate through sermons against theological norms to determine the relative faithfulness of the sermon. The chapter considers practical approaches for developing sermons that include material that has good opportunities to connect with people on all three settings through which people listen to sermons, and concludes with a sermon that is annotated to show how I attempted to incorporate ethos, logos, and pathos appeals.

Listener Preferences and Faithful Preaching

When we outlined some of these findings at the public conference to which reference was made in chapter 1, a perceptive lay listener made the following observation in a question-and-answer session: "You have done a good job describing what listeners want. But does that mean the preacher should give them what they want? What if what they want is unfaithful?" This listener raises an important issue for the preacher. Much of the data in this study is descriptive of how people listen, but a minister cannot stop with absorbing such data. For the preacher, of course, is called to interpret the gospel faithfully for the world of the congregation. The preacher cannot simply "give the people what they want" if what they want is theologically inappropriate. Preachers must consider the degree to which a listener comment reported in this study (or heard in another setting) is consistent or inconsistent with the deepest theological convictions of the denomination, congregation, and pastor.[1]

Each setting affords the preacher certain opportunities for correlating the gospel with persons in that setting. Each setting also raises cautions. By knowing qualities that enhance listening on each setting, a preacher may be able to shape the sermon so as to minimize a listener's initial resistance to the gospel and to enhance the possibility that the listener may take the sermon seriously. The preacher can also take advantage of points at which listener settings are already consistent with faithful values.

In the remarks that follow, I continue the pattern of the previous chapters by trying to let the listeners speak for themselves in bringing to the surface theological opportunities and cautions. I try to develop these ideas, as much as possible, from the practices of listening reflected in the interviewees' responses to our questions. I cite from comments from interviewees already cited in the book, but, as needed, I draw on other comments in the transcripts to deepen or fill out occasional points. From time to time I do point to opportunities or cautions that are not voiced in our particular interviews, but that have come to my attention through other interactions with listeners, preachers, and congregations.

Some Opportunities and Cautions for Preaching to Listeners on Ethos Settings

One of the distinguishing characteristics of listening through ethos settings is respect for the ordained office of the preacher. As one listener says, "A sermon has authority because the pastor preaches it." Such people perceive the preacher representing the accumulated wisdom of the church (symbolized by the ministerial office). A preacher could take advantage of such confidence in the sermon to venture bold interpretations of Christian faith and challenges to the community to witness.[2]

Listeners who honor the office of the preacher implicitly acknowledge that they are members of a tradition with a distinctive worldview. One listener notes that preaching plays an important role in helping the congregation identify this vision. "I think if we didn't have a sermon, then our thoughts, our boundary lines, begin to spread. For example, as any family, you need some kind of boundaries. Without a sermon, where we draw our boundaries may be further out and further out from what the Christian should be." This hearer acknowledges that the boundaries define both what Christians should and should not do. "It doesn't necessarily mean that what's preached in the service is all good and how we should follow this. It could be what we shouldn't be doing." Attitudes such as this listener's are an opportunity for the preacher to help the congregation name relationships and other things that are coherent with Christian values and those that are not.

Furthermore, the preacher could help such folk recognize a certain counter-cultural quality implicit in their respect for the ministerial office. By acknowledging the minister as representative of the Christian worldview, these listeners implicitly acknowledge that they do not singularly determine the meaning of their lives. A theological opportunity here is for the preacher to help people who hold this perception to recognize that such a view of person-in-community works against the rabid individualism so characteristic of North American culture. For these listeners do not see the isolated individual and her or his preferences as unilaterally determining what is meaningful. While the persons interviewed in our study sample did not use this language, a number of them recognize that the church is not simply an aggregate of individuals but, indeed, is a community. When an African American congregation is stirred, for instance, "You feel connected to other people when you see they have a similar response to the sermon...You realize when you hear a sermon, hey, you're not out there by yourself. This faith walk we have, we're all on common ground." Another listener remarked, "We all sort of come together and we know as we sit and listen to this message that we're all part of a bigger picture...I think it's nice to turn and to look at other people and to realize that we're all listening to this message at the same time, and that carries through the rest of the week." While the content of the message "carries through the rest of the week," the context clearly indicates that for this listener, the experience of community also "carries through."

Two cautions come with these initial characteristics. One is that congregations can develop a cult of the preacher in which their focus shifts from the gospel to making a quasi-idol of the preacher. Unfortunately, when talking about their histories as people who listen to sermons, some of the interviewees report preachers who apparently encourage such preacher-devotion, such as the preacher of whom our interviewee complained that the pastor is self-impressed. Indeed, this pastor "becomes bigger than what the pastor is doing." Another caution is that the preacher can misuse the authority of the office and can even become abusive. A number of interviewees, reflecting upon their histories of listening to sermons, recall preachers who misused the pulpit by belittling the congregation and otherwise disrespecting the people. A person who tunes into the sermon through ethos settings observes that when the preacher speaks with "an air of superiority," this listener begins to pay more attention to the aggravation caused by this "air" than to the content of the sermon.

Desire to regard the preacher as real is a related mark of congregants who participate in sermons through this setting. In particular, they are drawn to sermons in which preachers share their own struggles and otherwise demonstrate that preachers are "very much like us." A theological opportunity afforded to the preacher is to help the congregation become more attentive to their own "reality," especially to name and take seriously their own struggles. For instance, one of the persons interviewed in the study recalled the pastor speaking about how the pastor has worked with anger in the pastor's own life. Hearing the preacher struggle with how to deal with anger helped the parishioner become more attune to that parishioner's own anger, and helped the parishioner think about how to respond to anger in the parishioner's own life. Another parishioner told the story of hearing a person struggle with issues of faith in the pulpit and reflects, "To listen to another person openly and honestly witness to their own faith helps at times to connect and help me over a struggling point that I may have that they have already gone through, and now can help me get through."[3]

Another distinctive mark of approaching the sermon through ethos settings is concern for the integrity of the preacher in the pulpit and in life beyond the congregation. Such listeners want to believe that the preacher not only talks the talk, but walks the walk. "If you're going to preach against something and then you go out and do it, why am I going to listen to you the next day?" The preacher, of course, can urge the congregation towards their own integrity: being clear about what they believe, and living in ways that are consistent with those beliefs.

In this vein, admiration for the character of the preacher becomes, for some congregants, an occasion for the historic practice of imitation—modeling oneself after the kind of person who exemplifies the best in a tradition. "I could see the examples which they lived out in their lives." Another parishioner became involved in the community beyond the congregation, in part, because of the pastor's involvement. "It sort of rubs off on you."[4]

An opportunity afforded the preacher in connection with this concern is to help the congregation realize that concern for integrity is rooted in the integrity of God and is at the heart of the Jewish and Christian traditions. "Hear, O Israel: the Lord our God, the Lord is one" (Deut. 6:4, NIV). Israel can rely upon the promises of God because they are issued by One who is, by nature, trustworthy. For several listeners, the integrity and trustworthiness of the preacher represents the integrity of God; the people can count upon what the preacher says because the preacher should have integrity in the same manner as God. In a similar way, the preacher represents the kind of integrity that is also to characterize the life and witness of the congregation.

The interest in relationships that is associated with congregants who tune into the sermon through ethos settings provides two related theological opportunities for the preacher. First, it is an ideal point of entry to helping the congregation think theologically about relating with one another. As one interviewee says so eloquently, "Everyone has a relationship with everyone else." As a result, parishioners who listen on ethos settings recognize that they need to work at relating with one another in ways that are consistent with God's purposes, and many are receptive to the sermon to help them with this task. As one listener says, "The sermon should teach us to love one another." Another person remembers a sermon that prompted this person to repair broken relationships. The listener "had to go home and think about it a little more" but eventually "I mended my ways." Preachers can take advantage of this interest by urging members of the community to consider areas in their personal and corporate worlds that need change in order to more fully live out God's purposes.

Second, this interest is an opportunity for the preacher because God loves the world with unconditional love, and seeks not only relationships of love and justice among all peoples, but also for people to respond to the divine love with love for God. Consequently, members of the congregation need to relate with one another (and with folk outside the community) in loving and just patterns. As one of the interviewees said, when asked what the pastor is doing when standing up to preach, "I think that ideally the preacher is standing up to call together the people of God and to continue to form the community of God and to join people together as one in that act." This parishioner speaks for many who want to know how God wishes and empowers the members of the congregation to relate with one another (and to function) as community. Consequently, the preacher can often correlate the human interest in relationships with these divine desires by helping the congregation see that our positive experiences of relationship with one another help us understand God's relationship with us.

A caution here is that the preacher and congregation can let this concern for relationship be limited to the congregation and not be extended to the world beyond. In this latter case, not only might the congregation limit God's concern, but it can become ingrown, and relationships can sour. For example, a congregant recalled a time when a rural parish became almost hyper-focused on certain decisions regarding how to care for the parsonage (located next to the church building). The congregation became so polarized that, on Sunday morning, the factions would sit on opposite sides of the sanctuary, and the preacher would speak directly to the section containing the preacher's supporters (at least in this parishioner's memory), but would not speak directly to the antagonists. Consequently, this parishioner says to today's pastor, "Don't preach to one side of the room." This parishioner thinks the congregation is healthier now that they are working together on some projects in the village where the congregation is located.

Furthermore, many people with ethos orientations towards the sermon are interested in another outgrowth of relationship–reaching out to persons and communities beyond the congregation. This interest is a significant opportunity for the preacher to help people understand that such outreach is a part of the mission of the church and is intended to help bring about love and justice in as many circumstances as possible. The preacher can, perhaps, use this concern on the part of people who listen to the sermon through ethos settings to help them see the necessity of systemic change in the broader social world as means towards spreading the realm of positive relationships of love and justice. This theme comes through forcefully in several of the interviews. "I want a preacher…to show me a way to help. I believe in helping." This listener wants the minister to "show me how I can help or do things that would be an energizer where I can say, 'Oh yes. That would be something I can do.'" The preacher does not need to try to motivate such persons as much as provide suggestions for ways in which such folk can help.

Many congregants for whom ethos is the initial mode of hearing the sermon want the preacher to speak to them in their particularity as a community. Such people resist preachers who speak to them generically. When a visiting preacher mischaracterized a congregation, such a listener reflected more generally on that phenomenon, "Who are you? When it seems like the preachers are making some assumptions about the congregation that I feel are unfair, at that point I've already decided they don't know us, so why should I listen?" The opportunity, of course, is for the preacher to speak specifically about the interaction of the gospel with the congregation and its world. Such folk want to know what the sermon has to do with *us*.[5] With such folk, the preacher can often be quite pointed as to the implications of the gospel for the congregation and its context.

While none of our listeners directly raise this caution, it comes with the growing awareness of the systemic interrelatedness of all areas of life: A preacher can motivate a congregation to perform worthwhile, but limited, acts of love and justice that respond to human needs without tending to the underlying systemic causes of those problems. In fact, this point is one at which a preacher could take advantage of the trust that people have in the authority of the ministerial office to urge parishioners to think about the kinds of changes in social systems in North America, and around the globe, that are necessary to help the world community become a greater theater of love and justice.

People who listen to the sermon on ethos settings sometimes need to develop a clearer focus on the content of the sermon as theological content. They sometimes focus so much on the person of the preacher and on relationships in the community that they do not take advantage of how the ideas in the sermon can benefit the congregation.

Some Opportunities and Cautions for Preaching to People on Logos Settings

A distinctive mark of approaching the sermon through logos settings is the desire, even hunger on the part of some, for information and ideas. This inclination affords the preacher the opportunity to help such congregants move towards intellectual clarity about matters related to faith and ethics. I think of two points in particular at which the preacher might use this proclivity as a point of entry for engaging such listeners.

One is for developing as much precision as is possible around matters of doctrine and systematic theology. Several listeners in the study stated that they want to know as much as possible (given the limitations of human knowledge) what they can (and should) believe. As one listener says, since "only a limited number of people come to Sunday school," the sermon is "an opportunity for there to be some teaching about the Christian life and the Bible, and also maybe provide some material for thought relative to the Christian life during the week." Another interviewee says, "I'm concerned that people don't know a lot of times what they believe." Preachers need to help the congregation "be grounded in scripture" and in the historic affirmations of faith so that the congregation has a good foundation for everyday life and witness, especially when questions and tragedy befall. This listener was grateful for such grounding because when faced with a spouse's terminal illness, "I had something to count on." Indeed, a few auditors said that they became members of a particular congregation or denomination because of that community's theological positions. This interest in learning about core matters of Christian belief is an ideal opportunity to preach affirmations of faith and other ideas that are essential to the congregation's identity. How did these beliefs emerge in history? What were the critical questions they sought to answer? What can we make of such notions today?

Another opportunity area along the same line is to help these congregants develop a critical understanding of the Bible and its interpretation.[6] Many congregants in the pool interviewed for whom logos settings are primary, explicitly say they want to know more about how the Bible helps them make Christian sense of life. For example, "It, the Bible, is kind of like a history book. It tells you what happened, why it happened, and what the outcome was for the circumstances of what the people in Bible times did. I think that's for us—kind of giving us a warning as parents." But to understand the warnings (and other material in the Bible), interpretation is needed. The preacher can help the congregation towards fuller understandings (according to the theological tradition in which preacher and congregation move) of how to interpret texts from the Bible in their historical settings or how to determine their significance for today. The preacher can further help such listeners discern the relationship between texts in the Bible and the doctrine and systematic theology that power the congregation's theological identity.

A caution flag reminds us that preacher and congregation can get so caught up in thinking about these matters that they fail to move out in actual mission. While none of the people for whom logos is a portal into the sermon directly said that thinking about ideas related to Christian faith can become an end itself, fewer persons who listen on logos settings than on ethos settings spoke about the importance of the sermon leading to acts of mission. An interviewee sums up the goal of preaching for many persons on this setting by saying that the sermon should leave the congregation with something they can "reflect on." This preacher may need to help such persons remember that the faithful life includes not only faithful thinking but also faithful acts of witness in the congregation and in the larger world.

Many congregants who begin to listen to the sermon through logos settings are energized when the preacher provokes them to fresh thought. A listener holds out as a criterion for a good sermon the fact that "it helped somebody think." Another listener says, "For me, the sermon should open up an issue in a new way and give me insight." Another person points even more directly to the theological opportunity inherent in this quality of listening. "The preacher challenges your ways of thinking about the scripture that the preacher is addressing at the time. I call it my old way of saying about it. The preacher challenges that and causes you to think." Such people are ready for sermons to push them to consider ways of conceptualizing Christian faith that are fresh to them. The preacher can be fairly bold with such hearers, recognizing, of course, that since they are independent thinkers they will come to their own conclusions regarding the ideas that the preacher advances.

Another distinguishing characteristic of listening through logos settings is a hunger to know the meaning of life. An example that recurs in several of the interviews is voiced with precision by one listener. "Why do we suffer?" This listener believes that the answer cannot be fully known until we "get to heaven," but in the meantime, this person yearns for theological reflection that will help make bearable sense of this subject. The opportunity, of course, is for the sermon to engage in one of the oldest and most important functions of religion: to help listeners make sense of experience from the perspective of the transcendent. As is well known, the Latin root of the word religion (*religare*) means "to bind together." The preacher can perform a much-appreciated logos function by helping the congregation understand how the various pieces of life fit together.

A caution is that the hunger for a settled understanding of life in these chaotic and stressful times can sometimes allow pastors and parishioners to settle for perspectives on meaning that do not take full account of the possibilities available. In so doing, they overlook possibilities that may more fully explain the nature of God and the world. The questions in the interviews did not attempt to solicit the listeners' views on specific theological topics, but listeners occasionally refer to those views while illustrating their responses to sermons. Many (though not all) of the theological views that come to expression in the survey reflect popular Christian piety similar to that articulated in religious broadcasting.[7] For example, a number of interviewees refer to misfortunes, difficulties, and tragedies in life as things that God controls. Some listeners believe that an omnipotent God wills these things for specific purposes. The job of the preacher and the listener (from this point of view) is to try to figure out the purpose, or, if that is not possible, to learn to live with the effects of the misfortune, vaguely trusting that it was "God's will" and that we cannot fully understand it in this present life. They adopt a kind of functional Stoicism in which the goal is simply to bear up under the suffering. To be sure, our survey did not invite reflection on this topic. However, few of the people who brought it up to illustrate aspects of preaching indicated being aware of other theological resolutions to the theological questions raised by difficulty, misfortune, and tragedy. This caution (people sometimes settle too quickly for explanations that are clear but not fully satisfactory) turns out to be another opportunity for the preacher: to offer folk more theologically adequate interpretations.

Desire for order in the sermon and for signs of careful preparation are marks of congregants who participate in sermons through this setting. The opportunity here is to push the preacher to be as clear as possible about what the preacher wants to say. As an interviewee says:

> I have no tolerance for things that are ill-presented…The sermon needs to have a thought progression where I can see and hear the stories being told and how they fit together. If I pay attention well enough, I should understand by the end how it relates to the beginning and that there was a thought process involved. I need to see the logic. I need to see the flow.

Other listeners stress that it is important for them to get the point (or the points) of the sermon. Even when the preacher has not come to a conclusion, it is important to these listeners to have a clear grasp of the issues and the stakes involved. To do so means that preachers need to undertake thorough preparation of the sermon.

A caution comes not from the interviews, but from hearing student preachers and established pastors describe their typical methods of sermon preparation. The desire for order in preparation, as well as in the sermon itself, can sometimes limit the preacher's openness to fresh insights along the way. The questions and resources that a preacher asks and uses may preclude interacting with other questions and resources. The preacher may not know what to do with insights and resources that come into the world of sermon preparation outside the preacher's usual patterns of preparation and organization. Not knowing where to fit them in, the preacher may set them aside and not deal with them. The problem of rigidity of focus is compounded when preachers have waited until late in the week to begin the preparation of the sermon and do not have time to look at the text, topic, or circumstances through a fresh angle of vision. To be of optimum value to listeners who are challenged by fresh perspectives, ministers should develop habits of sermon preparation that can incorporate unexpected perspectives and that allow time to consider them.

The interest in comparing and contrasting various ways of interpreting important matters that are associated with congregants who participate in the sermon through logos settings provides two theological opportunities for the preacher. One is to help congregations think through those specific issues. One of our listeners, for instance, reflected on the help a sermon gave in struggling with how to respond to the destruction of the World Trade Towers. "What good will it do us to go over and take ten, twenty, or fifty thousand lives? What good did it do us over in Hiroshima to kill whatever it was, seventy-five thousand in the first day, or something like that, by dropping the A-Bomb? What does that accomplish for our Christian mission?" Persons who hear the sermon on logos settings are eager for the preacher to bring such pointed reasoning to bear on many topics.

The other theological opportunity is to model patterns of comparing and contrasting ideas and their merits in ways that people can use when thinking about other issues in life from a theological point of view. After recalling a potentially explosive issue in a congregation (whether women could serve as leaders in the congregation), a listener notes that the preacher said, "Here are the facts. Here are the positives of it. Here are the negatives of it as I understand them. Now you really need to deal with these two facts and come out with a conclusion." The preacher clarified the issues, the pros and the cons, and stated the preacher's own opinion and gave reasons for it. The listener was glad to know the position of the preacher, but was even more benefited by the preacher's methodology, which provided this listener with a way to think through the issue.

A listener caution that goes along this approach: The preacher can leave the impression that decisions regarding significant theological and ethical issues are completely relative. "There is a danger there of watering down a message by simply laying the pluses and minuses out there and saying, 'Now it's up to you to determine what you should be doing.'" To be sure, a preacher needs to acknowledge that, since all human awareness is finite, all judgments contain within them a degree of relativity. Nevertheless, preachers do need to help the congregation recognize how particular decisions are consistent or inconsistent with the community's theological tradition and norms.

Congregants who listen to the sermon through logos settings often have a low awareness of the presence of feeling in themselves, the congregation, and larger world. Many such listeners are suspicious of feeling and its role in coming to decisions. Feeling, to such listeners, is ephemeral and subjective, and does not provide real criteria for making decisions, and taking action. The opportunity for the preacher is to encourage the congregation to as much clarity as possible regarding issues at stake in ideas, and decisions and consequences. Such listeners are eager for this very thing. For instance, after being moved by hearing a missionary speak about the difficulties faced by people in another land, a hearer responds, "Wow. I hadn't realized. I didn't realize. If I were in that setting, do I have the fortitude? If I were in that setting, would I rise to the occasion?" The preacher can help this listener by reflecting on the meaning of the feeling generated by the touching story.

A potential caution is that such preachers and congregations can overlook important motifs that arise from the life of feeling, and from people who approach the world through feeling. The interviews did not turn up (to my knowledge) comments from listeners that reveal instances of hiding from emotions. While it is true that "your emotions will lie to you," as one of the interviewees says, one must wonder if, even for such persons, feeling sometimes signals trans-verbal awareness.

The preacher may need to help some persons who listen to the sermon through logos settings pay more attention to the theological implications of the character and integrity of the preacher. The preacher may occasionally need to help these people also occasionally recognize the importance of relating in meaningful ways with other people in the congregation. Sermons might also prompt people who listen to sermons through logos ears to become more attuned to their own feelings and to the importance of feelings in others.

Some Opportunities and Cautions for Preaching to People on Pathos Settings

A characteristic mark of approaching the sermon through pathos settings is to perceive feeling not only as a passing function of physiology but as a realm of knowledge. For instance, one of the listeners described a sermon as having authority "When it speaks to your heart and you feel that it is something that's moved you. You're filled. . I can't put words quite on it." An opportunity here is for preaching both to feed and to interpret (conceptually) this realm, and listeners are often grateful when ministers perform this function. A listener responded to the destruction of the Word Trade Center in New York in 2001 with feelings that "you just can't get out." After expressing gratitude that the preachers provided names for the feelings evoked by the tragedy at the twin towers, this listener generalizes, "Sometimes the ministers can hit on that and help you come up with the words." Being aware of the "words" allows this listener to deal with feelings in ways that are more satisfactory than when the feelings remain unnamed, but are still very powerful.

A caution is that such preacherly explanations may sound partial, reductionistic, not quite on the mark, and even shallow to the person who listens through pathos settings. After a sermon in class that contained a deep pathos moment, one student said to another who had tried to say what the moment meant in propositional language, "You're trying, but you just don't quite get it." To be sure, a preacher cannot interpret such feelings in an entirely satisfactory way in conventional language; however, the opportunity is present for the preacher to place such feelings in larger frameworks of meaning.

Nevertheless, for the sake of those moments in life when feelings are simply not enough (even for these folk), the preacher can help them move towards naming their powerful emotional experiences in theological terms.

By definition, of course, ministers cannot program the lives of feeling in the congregation. Yet, by including material in the sermon that touches the intuitive realm (e.g., stories, images, material from the life of the preacher) and is theologically appropriate, the preacher can help the congregation strengthen strains in the life of feeling that are associated with the gospel. Such sermons can help listeners develop unspoken, but powerful, associations with faithful values and actions to which they can respond positively when encountered in other sermons and, more importantly, in life settings outside the sanctuary.

When hearing content in the sermon that speaks to the realm of emotional knowledge, parishioners who synthesize the sermon through pathos settings often learn to respond to people and situations intuitively in ways that are suggested by the sermon. After commenting on a sense of emotional response to the preacher, one person says, "There's also that emotional connection with connecting the congregation with issues or with the world and seeing both of those in the light of faith and what we can do about that." The listener recalls a situation in which the church treasurer had embezzled some money from the congregation. The preacher said, "Yes, there's been a loss. We need to grieve our losses. We need to be gentle and kind and understanding, and we need to stand our ground." This listener responded to the embezzlement with a combination of gentleness, kindness, and understanding. Although our interview questions did not probe the effects of such intuitive awareness on the listener's perceptions of the world outside the sanctuary, it is reasonable to suppose that when their feelings have been touched in theologically appropriate ways during the sermon, they may watch the evening news (and take part in other activities beyond the church) and respond intuitively in theologically appropriate ways to policy decisions, revelations of injustice, international events, and other matters.

A caution is that emotional associations, even when rooted deep within the emotional life of the self and the community, do not always occur in ways that are theologically appropriate. The intuitive life can be wrong, just as ideas can be. A complicating difficulty is that whereas propositional knowledge is out in the open for critical evaluation, awareness in the life of feeling is much more difficult to evaluate. Indeed, not only is this realm of knowledge hard to discuss (and therefore to evaluate critically), but it can be circular. "I just feel that something is true." "Why do you feel that it is true?" "I don't know. I just do." Preachers need to help such folk develop criteria by which to distinguish emotional associations that are consistent with the gospel from those that are not. As we pointed out above, a few of the people for whom pathos settings are a port of entry into the sermon recognize the need for such criteria. One person notices that "God is a God of love, not of hate," and is a God who seeks to deliver people from bondage and to support diversity. The listener concludes that texts, doctrines, or actions that express love and promise deliverance and support diversity are consistent with God's purposes, while texts, doctrines, or actions that work against those things are not. The preacher needs to help other people for whom pathos settings are ports of entry into the sermon to recognize the need for such criteria and to learn how to name and employ such standards.

Two cautions come to mind in this regard. One is that the preacher can manipulate the feelings of others.[8] For instance, one listener says straightforwardly, "Emotions, I feel in the church when in the context of sermons, are often abused. I think that sometimes a minister will use emotions. They use emotions as buttons to push people to make them accept one particular idea or to actually turn them off of something else." This congregant was particularly distressed because such a preacher had not only emotionally manipulated the congregation with a story, but lied about its truthfulness, and thus violated one of the fundamental requirements of ethos: honesty. While we typically think of manipulation in a bad way (e.g. getting people to do things that benefit the preacher or the church but that are not consistent with responsible theological norms), a preacher can also manipulate people for good ends such as supporting a mission project. However, manipulation is still manipulation, and a preacher should want people to take up certain ideas or behaviors with a recognition of what they are turning towards and away from, and why.

Another caution that is possible at this juncture is that the emotional experience of hearing a sermon could become an end in itself.[9] I offer this caution hesitantly because the transcripts do not directly confirm it. However, when speaking about the purpose of preaching, listeners who approach the message through pathos settings tend to speak largely in terms of being "uplifted," "filled," "touched," "inspired," "quickened," and "convicted," as well as "feeling refreshed" and "feeling good." When a listener who thinks that the sermon "helps you find your spirituality" imagines "spirituality" only as a private, interior, emotional experience, guidance is needed to help that person realize larger, more social aspects of spirituality. Only a handful of persons in this hearing cohort speak of the sermon "getting you on your feet" to act in mission or to take up other Christian practices that are focused outside the self and on the congregation or world. If this impression is even partially correct, the preacher needs to help such listeners remember that the purposes of the sermon (and other aspects of the congregation's life) include prompting the congregation towards acts of mission, critical reflection, and other attitudes and actions that are part of the raison d'etre of the church.

Willingness to consider feelings of discomfort as an occasion for self-reflection is associated with folk who receive the sermon through pathos settings. This provides a theological opportunity for the preacher to help guide the congregation in this very act and to propose possible responses. The preacher can help people name their discomfort in theological terms, the reasons for it, and identify points at which such emotional distress indicates reasons for change. For example, one of our interviewees vividly called certain kinds of sermons "squirmers," that is, sermons that cause the congregation to "squirm" because of a contradiction between Christian values and congregational attitudes or actions. For example, one squirmer prompted the congregation to recognize "how blessed we are, and yet, at the same time, how selfish for not sharing more of what we've got." Other squirmers called attention to how the congregation treated street people, how people carry grudges, when people in the congregation needed to practice forgiveness. "You don't want to admit it, but it's there." An opportunity is here for the preacher to develop sermons designed to cause squirming around issues that are important to the congregation, the wider world, and the gospel. For instance, the preacher could encourage members in the congregation to recognize their discomfort aroused by pictures, stories, and information about homelessness as occasion to repent of values and actions that prolong systemic causes of homelessness. Listeners for whom pathos settings are the bands through which they receive the sermon are typically not put off by such squirming. On the contrary, they recognize it as an occasion for growth. Most preachers could probably move much more forcefully in this direction.

Several people whose initial mode of hearing the sermon is through pathos settings report that they weep from time to time in worship (and in other public places). Some seem quite comfortable doing so. Others feel a little awkward. The preacher has a theological opportunity to assure folk that tears in the sanctuary are quite acceptable. The pastor can correlate crying in worship with the gospel. As an expression of God accepting all unconditionally, the congregation accepts people who weep during sermons. Congregants can be free to express their deepest selves in the sacred assembly, and, thereby, to experience something of God's acceptance.

Several interviewees who tune into the homily through pathos settings report that they are moved by stories that function not just as illustrations of points but as narrative worlds. This proclivity provides the preacher with an opportunity to tell such stories. For these folk, the experience of hearing the story is itself a part of the meaning of the story. A caution, of course, is that the preacher needs to tell such stories well, and listeners themselves suggest some things that preachers can do in this regard. One person says, "You need to engage the whole person–the mind, the senses, the smell, the hearing, the eyes." Another person notices that stories need to give people opportunities to refract their own experience through the story. The congregation has two pastors.

> The pastors use very descriptive language. They build...They know a lot about the nuances that the language, that the words themselves may create when we're sitting here listening to them. We're all going to get different interpretations from one particular word, and that's okay because it helps the preachers reach us without having to say, "You feel this way. You feel this way." The preacher uses a word in such a way that we all connect to that word.

The preacher needs to use language vividly to create the scene, characters, and the plot. Like a good short story or novel, a story in a sermon should "build," that is, have a plot and tension that moves towards a climax. For the person who listens to the sermon on pathos settings, the preacher needs to be careful not to over-explain the story by saying things like, "You feel this way." The preacher needs to leave some space in and around the story for the congregation to recognize their own connections with the story.[10]

People who usually listen to the sermon on pathos settings say that the preacher's embodiment can contribute to stirring them (or leaving them unaffected). To be sure, different listeners and different congregations speak of different approaches or styles of embodiment that they find moving. Regardless of whether one is touched by a more exuberant style or by one that is quieter but no less intense, most hearers in this part of the study would agree with the one who said, "I want to feel that the minister is engaged. I don't want to feel like we're listening to a book being read. I want to have the sense that this is meaningful to them, too." Another listener interprets the preacher showing emotion in the pulpit as a sign that the preacher is learning the very lesson that the preacher is giving through the sermon. This viewpoint gives the preacher the opportunity to speak in the pulpit with passion that is appropriate to the preacher's own sense of self, the subject matter, and the congregational culture. A caution, obviously, is that feeling the preacher expresses in the pulpit must be genuine. As one listener said, "I don't believe in theatrical performances in the pulpit." When the congregation thinks that the preacher is "performing," people tend to be suspicious.

I expected that the interviews of people who enter the sermon through pathos channels would reveal that these folk are especially sensitive to the feelings of other people. I expected that they would say they often feel their own deep versions of the joy and pain of others. There are a few such references in the interviews. One listener speaks of being moved by a preacher's description of working conditions at a national retailer, and joining a boycott of that company in support of better treatment for its employees. The sermon caused the listener to feel the pain of the workers, and the listener responded with resolve to end that pain. Another member of a congregation reports hearing a touching sermon on financial giving that prompted this person (and others) to increase their financial support of the congregation. Still another listener reported changing behavior after hearing a sermon that depicted the hurt caused to other people by certain behavior and realizing that this listener engaged in that very behavior. "You don't want to leave no hurt nowhere." However, these interviewees speak more about their own feelings than about their feelings for other people or about the feelings of other people.[11] Nevertheless, the preacher might view the sensitivity of these folk to the life of feeling as opportunity to encourage these listeners to consider how other people feel about the world and to respond appropriately. For example, the preacher might invite such listeners to feel the pain of those suffering injustice and to act to relieve that pain by witnessing against injustice and for justice. Such associations could empower mission.

Like people who listen to the sermon on ethos settings, those who enter the world of the sermon through pathos settings sometimes need to attend more closely to the ideas and information in the sermon. From time to time, some such listeners are so mesmerized by the life of feeling that they do not recognize how theological ideas can help them interpret their interior lives, as well as become points of connection with the feelings of others.

Three Settings and One Sermon

In the chapters that precede, I have mentioned, along the way, ideas about how ministers can take account of each setting of listening in preaching. However, it may be helpful to discuss these specific profiles with a broad spectrum of approaches that a preacher may take, always keeping in mind the fact that each listener and each congregation is a particular combination of listening tendencies.[12] Pastors can determine which approaches have more or less potential for particular congregations through pastoral listening to the congregation to discern the patterns of the listening fields in the community and the needs of the congregation at the time of a given sermon or season of preaching.[13]

The key proposal here is that a pastor can incorporate into every (or nearly every) sermon material that parishioners are likely to receive and process on each of the three settings. To put it crudely, the preacher could communicate the message in three languages in each sermon—ethos language, logos language, and pathos language. In one sermon, the preacher could say the same thing in these three different modes.

Diagnostic Table

In preparation for a sermon, the preacher could ask simple diagnostic questions to determine the degree to which the sermon contains material that the congregation is likely to receive positively. A preacher could also create a table that shows how the preacher appeals to each of the three major settings over time. To help the preacher incorporate significant aspects of congregational culture, ethos, logos, pathos, and embodiment, Table 1 is a chart that enables a preacher to identify the degree to which these appeals appear in a single sermon, and to track the degree to which they come to expression in sermons over a season of preaching.[14] A preacher can then increase or decrease the emphases on particular qualities. A preacher can, of course, develop a similar chart for all seasons of the year.[15]

Pastoral listening may lead a minister to conclude that a particular congregational setting needs particular emphasis in preaching. Consequently, a preacher might develop a sermon or a series of sermons with that setting in mind. For example, a pastor may conclude that a congregation needs to understand the theological rationale for a particular church practice.

Table 1

Tracking Appeals to Persons Who Hear Sermons through Different Settings over a Season of Preaching

In the boxes below, a preacher could note the elements of the sermon that take account of congregational context and that appeal to persons who listen to the sermon through different settings through one season of the Christian year. Keeping such a chart over time encourages the preacher to notice the degree to which sermons contain elements that appeal to the spectrum of listeners and to add or reduce emphases as needed. The preacher can create other charts for other seasons—Advent, Christmas, Easter, and segments of Ordinary Time. Preachers whose sermons are determined by free selection of scripture texts or topics can create such a chart over periods of six to twelve weeks (or some other length of time).

	Ash Wed.	1st Sun. Lent	2nd Sun. Lent	3rd Sun. Lent	4th Sun. Lent	5th Sun. Lent	Palm/Pas.Sun.	Easter
What material in the sermon reflects congregational culture? (a concern to consider in all three settings and embodiment)								
What ethos appeals are in the sermon?								
What logos appeals are in the sermon?								
What pathos appeals are in the sermon?								
What aspects of the embodiment have a good chance of engaging the congregation?								

CHAPTER 6

An Example: A Sermon on Luke 3:7–18

When discussing the ideas in this book with ministers and students, the question nearly always comes up, "Can you give us an example? What can we do in actual sermons to try to engage people such as Ethel, Lorenzo, and Pat?" In this chapter I describe my own process from thinking about Luke 3:7–18 to developing a sermon on that text as a guest preacher in December, 2003.[1] The first part of the chapter describes the congregational context, and offers a brief exegesis of the text and a summary of the direction of the sermon. The chapter then names characteristics of each of the three settings to which a preacher might appeal when developing a sermon on this passage. I respond to the questions posed in Table 1, "What ethos appeals...logos appeals...pathos appeals...(will be) in this sermon?" The sermon itself follows, and is annotated to show how the principles articulated in the reflection come to expression in the sermon.

Congregational Context

The text below appears in the Revised Common Lectionary on the Third Sunday of Advent in Year C. I was asked to preach on this passage in an Episcopal congregation whose pastor is a good friend. The congregation contains many well-educated upper-middle-class persons of non-Hispanic European origin, and is located in an older suburb of Indianapolis near a major thoroughfare, not far from two major cross streets with small businesses and restaurants. I try to speak specifically to some aspects of the congregation's setting that are known to me, taking into account the Advent season with its theme of preparation.

The Text

(7) John said to the crowds that came out to be baptized by him, "You brood of vipers. Who warned you to flee from the wrath to come? (8) Bear fruits worthy of repentance. Do not begin to say to yourselves, 'We have Abraham as our ancestor' for I tell you, God is able from these stones to raise up children to Abraham. (9) Even now the ax is lying at the root of the trees; every tree therefore that does not bear good fruit is cut down and thrown into the fire.

(10) And the crowds asked him, "What then should we do?" (11) In reply [John] said to them, "Whoever has two coats must share with anyone who has none; and whoever has food must do likewise." (12) Even tax collectors came to be baptized, and they asked him, "Teacher, what should we do?" (13) He said to them, "Collect no more than the amount prescribed for you." (14). Soldiers also asked him, "And we, what should we do?" He said to them, "Do not extort money from anyone by threats or false accusation, and be satisfied with your wages."

(15) As the people were filled with expectation, and all were questioning in their hearts concerning John, whether he might be the Messiah, (16) John answered all of them by saying, "I baptize you with water; but one who is more powerful than I is coming; I am not worthy to untie the thong of his sandals. He will baptize you with the Holy Spirit and fire. (17) His winnowing fork is in his hand to clear his threshing floor and to gather the wheat into his granary; but the chaff he will burn with unquenchable fire."(18) So with many other exhortations, [John] proclaimed good news to the people.

Brief Exegesis

Luke, whose theology was influenced by apocalypticism, believed that God would soon end the present, evil age and replace it with a new realm of peace, justice and love, often called the realm (NRSV: kingdom) of God.[2] Luke interpreted the event of Jesus Christ as a sign that this great transformation was beginning and would be completed by an apocalypse (the return of Jesus). The church was called to demonstrate the character of the new realm in its life and to invite others to prepare for the realm.

Nearly every passage in the gospel of Luke and the book of Acts contains multiple themes, any one of which could be the center point of a sermon. Because Advent is a season of preparation for the coming of Christ, both at

Christmas and at the final apocalypse, and because repentance is both a traditional means of preparation and a leading motif in Luke 3:7–18, I decided to focus on that aspect of the text for the sermon. For Luke, as for the Jewish tradition that Luke presumes, repentance is the act of turning away from collusion with the old age and of turning towards the divine realm. An act of repentance is a sign of commitment to living in God's ways and an act of preparation for the new age.

A community should repent of all things that work against God's purposes of blessing for all, including economic exploitation, other forms of injustice and repression, and violence. Luke 3:7–18, especially vv. 10–14, evokes several of these themes. I am surprised at one Lukan turn in the notion of repentance. For Luke, a person who has two coats is to repent by giving one coat to a person who has none, and the same with food. These actions are not charitable donation, but are acts of repentance. By retaining two coats when a person needs only one, that person is not only denying a coat to someone who does not have one, but does not trust in God either to complete the manifestation of the divine realm soon enough that the second coat will not be needed or to provide a replacement coat if the apocalypse is delayed. Hanging onto the second coat is a means of trying to shore up one's own security while not trusting God to provide. Those who do not share, but hoard wealth, face a caustic judgment (e.g., Lk. 12:13–21, 16:19–31; Acts 5:1–11). In Acts 2:42–47 and 4:32–37 we learn that repentance with respect to material goods means putting one's resources at the service of the community so that all in the community have the resources for a life of blessing. This theme permeates the gospel of Luke and the book of Acts.[3]

Many scholars think that some members of the Lukan church had not repented wholeheartedly. They were not sharing their material resources but were hoarding them (perhaps because they did not trust God to provide materially for them until the apocalypse). They may have welcomed repentant tax collectors and soldiers into their midst without requiring the latter to end their gouging, extortion, threats, and false accusations.[4]

Luke portrays John the Baptist as a prophet in continuity with the classical prophets of Israel who attempted to alert the people to the community's injustice, idolatry, and other violations of the covenant that would bring divine judgment upon the community, as well as call people to repent as a prelude to restoration.[5] According to Luke 3:7–9, the crowd that has gathered to hear John is aware that the apocalyptic judgment is imminent and they seek to escape it. By calling them a brood of vipers, however, John accused them not only of insincere repentance but of colluding with the snake who tempted the first human pair in Genesis 3:1–7. According to John, they relied on the covenant that God made to Abraham and Sarah without recognizing that each generation must live covenantally with one another, that is, in a community that takes care of the needs of all.

John used the fierce image of cutting down a tree and throwing it into the fire to impress upon the hearers the fact that the apocalypse and its fearful consequences were upon them.

Like many crowds in Luke-Acts, when this one was confronted by the claims of God, they asked the question, "What then should we do?" Luke thereby suggests that the reader ask the same question. In vv. 11–14, John specifies the content of repentance. Those who have resources typified by two coats and abundant food are to repent by sharing with those who have none. Many preachers today regret that Luke does not admonish the tax collectors and soldiers to renounce their vocations. Tax collectors, after all, not only gouged the people by charging exorbitantly, but financed repression on the part of Herod and the Romans. Soldiers kept the idolatrous and oppressive Roman government in power. Although Luke does not counsel the tax collectors and soldiers to walk away from their jobs, Luke foresees God replacing all repressive social structures in the near future with the divine real. John's exhortation to the tax collectors and the soldiers is an interim measure: Luke seeks to ameliorate the suffering of the population between John's preaching and the apocalypse by counseling the tax collectors to charge "only the amount prescribed for you" and the soldiers not to extort by violence and to "be satisfied with your wages."

In vv. 15–18, Luke makes it clear that while John was rightly preparing people for the imminent apocalypse, another person will be God's agent in effecting the cosmic transformation. John prepares a community for the new age through baptism. The one who comes afterwards will unleash the Holy Spirit and fire. For Luke, the Spirit empowers the manifestation of the divine realm during Jesus' ministry and continues that manifestation through the church after Jesus' ascension.[6] The fire is the apocalyptic judgment when God will separate the wheat from the chaff and consign the latter to "burn with unquenchable fire."

The sermon below is based on an analogy between people in the world of Luke and attitudes and actions today.[7] Many people in the contemporary congregation, like many in Luke's world, do not fully repent. We are complicit in things that work against God's purposes, including hanging onto excessive quantities of material resources while many people in the world are in need. In the sermon, I intended to develop a focus on repentance during the Advent season as sharing fiscal and physical means with the community, especially the poor, so that all may experience as much blessing as possible within the present broken age of history, and so that we would be relieved of the burdens of greed and of idolatry of wealth.[8]

When we share a second coat with someone who is without one, we turn away from self-preservation and turn towards a world that is moving towards the realm of God in its provision of abundance for all. Because Advent is a season in which people are preparing for Christmas by paying attention to the material things they will give and receive, I decided to give this theme a prominent place in the sermon.

Luke does not deal directly with a matter of concern to today's church: congregational and denominational initiatives in social and systemic change. Of particular importance for the themes in Luke 3:7–18 are changes in social and economic systems that keep people in (and benefiting from) poverty. Luke was confident that the apocalypse would effect what today's preacher calls "systemic change," for the apocalypse would mean a complete regeneration of all social systems. The sermon below does not have time to focus on that subject in detail, but does acknowledge that while individual repentance is important, social and systemic reconstruction is needed.[9] In the meantime, the community is to live in the world without being overwhelmed by present false values (such as greed) and by witnessing to God's purposes of blessing for all.

Planning the Sermon to Appeal to Each Setting

The preacher typically wants to appeal to ethos, logos, and pathos settings in a sermon from the perspective of congregational culture. I now highlight some things I considered taking into account in the sermon that, I thought, would have a good chance of engaging people on each setting. I say "*considered* taking into account" because one sermon seldom gives the preacher enough time to include every insight in one sermon.

Appeals to Ethos

With respect to traditional internal ethos, although I normally lead worship and preach in a suit, I hoped to create a positive visual impression with the congregation by wearing an alb and a stole per the habit of ministers in the congregation, and I tried to follow clergy custom in the chancel (e.g., pausing in front the altar when entering and exiting). I tried to use language that an educated upper-middle-class congregation could easily follow.[10] I also included some material in the sermon to indicate that I live in a world that is similar to that of the congregation so that they would recognize me as "one of them." A collect from the liturgy for the day ("Stir up your power, O God...") provided not only an ideal thematic connection to the sermon but also an opportunity to develop internal ethos by using material that the congregation assumes to be authoritative. I preach from a manuscript, but I tried to get the sermon into my head so that I would not "read it off the page" (as one of the interviewees said).

With respect to traditional motifs of external ethos, I expected that since I was associated in a positive way with their minister, they would project onto me some of their high regard for him. Prior to the services, I joined the minister in the hallway leading into the worship space to greet people as they entered. People seemed to respond positively to a firm handshake and a warm smile. I tried to pick up a sense of how people in the congregation were feeling and some of the questions and issues of concern to them. Nearly everyone mentioned the capture of the former President of Iraq, Saddam Hussein, that had taken place just a few hours earlier, and that I learned about on National Public Radio only a couple of hours before. I did not have time to think through a disciplined theological reflection on the meaning of that event, but I could tell from the comments in the hallway that it was much on people's minds and that I needed to acknowledge it in the sermon.

For persons who tune into the sermon on ethos settings, the integrity of the preacher is a core value. This value came especially into play around a theological issue. As noted in the "Brief Exegesis" above, Luke believed that God would end the present world and complete the manifestation of the divine realm through a dramatic apocalyptic cataclysm. Concern for integrity compelled me, as a revisionary theologian, to indicate in the sermon that I do not share this view. However, since this sermon did not primarily focus on eschatology, I could not dwell on this point. I tried to phrase that concern in such a way as to respect others in the congregation who hold a form of apocalyptic eschatology.

It is easy to be "real" when preaching on this text. I recognized immediately a range of responses to John the Baptist that could come into the sermon: I am both put off and fascinated by the fact that John is pictured so differently from most religious leaders today. Further, I have the same kinds of questions, anxieties, and hopes as the crowd that heard John and as Luke's community, and I suspected that the congregation did, too. The personal experience of the preacher is of interest to many congregants who listen to the sermon through ethos settings, so I do refer to some of my own questions, anxieties, hopes, and views.[11]

Relationship is important both to congregants who listen to the sermon on ethos settings and to the world of this text. Luke urges people to repent out of pastoral concern. By appealing to the notion of sharing, Luke invokes the Jewish motif of covenant, which implies that people are related with one another. Although a preacher should avoid anachronism (the practice of reading a contemporary concern into an ancient text when that concern is not found in the text), I remembered the interviewee who commented that "everyone has a relationship with everyone else." The message makes explicit the theme that people should share because we are in covenantal relationship with God and with one another. This idea relates directly to another that is important to parishioners who begin to listen to the sermon through ethos settings— reaching out to the world beyond the congregation.

Many congregants for whom ethos settings are the band on which they listen to sermons are eager to know how the sermon relates to the particularity of their congregation. Being a guest, I tried to ascertain from the minister points of connection between the direction of the sermon and the congregation. I also looked around the building and listened to comments from parishioners in the hallway before the service.

Appeals to Logos

When thinking about the interest of the person who approaches the sermon through logos settings, I was aware of the vast amount of information that could fascinate such listeners in a sermon on this text. These matters include the historical, political, and economic situation of the world of the first century; how scholars reconstruct the situation within and around Luke's congregation; the dramatic figure of John the Baptist; first century apocalyptic theology; how the themes of this passage are amplified later in the gospel of Luke and in the book of Acts; and the relationship of the Lukan congregation to Judaism implied in this passage, not to mention the meaning of the many details within the text–brood of vipers, fruits worthy of repentance, the role of Abraham and Sarah, the image of the axe cutting down the tree and throwing it into the fire, the significance of the coat, the work of tax collectors and soldiers and how Jewish people in antiquity perceived these figures, the term "Messiah" and its place in Luke-Acts, the significance of John's baptism, the image of John not being worthy to untie the thong of the Messiah's sandals, baptism by the Holy Spirit, fire, the image of winnowing, and the unquenchable fire.

There are too many details in the text to consider them all in a single sermon of twelve to fifteen minutes. Indeed, several of these aspects of the text could, by themselves, become the foci of sermons. For this sermon, one idea in the text is pivotal: repentance. I sought to define repentance clearly as the act of turning away from collusion with the old age, turning towards the divine realm, and as a sign of commitment to living in God's ways and as preparation for the new age.

Since the persons who begin to listen to the sermon through logos settings are often intrigued by new ideas, as well as ideas that stretch and challenge them, I pondered whether there were aspects of Luke's notion of repentance that might seem fresh, even challenging, to the congregation. When I thought about my prior history with the word "repentance," I realized that I have often thought of repentance mainly in terms of feeling sorry for misdeeds, whereas Luke proposes a larger, more positive, and dynamic point of view; one that involves ethical action. It occurred to me that my own change of thinking might be a mirror for a similar change in perspective on the part of the congregation.

As a result of leading many Bible studies in local congregations, I have found that participants are seldom aware that the gospel of Luke and the book of Acts tell a continuous story, and that when interpreting a text from the gospel of Luke, one should follow its themes into the Acts (and when interpreting a text from the Acts, one should trace its themes in their origins and development in the gospel of Luke). I thought that some listeners would be interested in a connection between Luke 3:7–18 and Luke's picture of the early church as a community of provision through sharing in the Acts of the Apostles.

Listeners for whom logos settings are a port of entry into the sermon like to get a clear idea of the major point(s) of the sermon, and for the sermon to unfold in an orderly way. I planned for the whole sermon to cohere around the idea that God graciously makes it possible for us to prepare for both Christmas and the realm of God by a Lukan-style repentance. The approach to repentance involves sharing fiscal and physical means with the community so that all may experience as much blessing as possible within the present broken age of history and so that we will be relieved of the burdens of greed and of idolatry of wealth. To get to this point in the sermon, I decided to follow the narrative of the text, explaining aspects of the historical and literary setting, and details within the text that would lead to the discovery of this point as a major point of the text and of the sermon. After that point was expressed in the sermon, I decided to consider a theological question about it (how does God help us repent?) and some practical implications (how can the community engage in Lukan-style acts of repentance?).

Hearers in the logos-listening cohort also want to know how the ideas of the sermon might affect them. I made a decision to focus more on how the congregation and its members could engage in particular hands-on acts of repentance that would be of direct and immediate benefit to people in the world of the congregation. I decided to mention some actions that I knew the congregation was already taking (e.g., collecting food, clothing, Christmas presents, money) and to suggest some opportunities that went beyond what they were already doing (such as donating blood, working in a homeless shelter). I wanted to help the congregation see that such actions need not be simply donations, but can represent acts of repentance: turning away from self-preservation and turning towards preserving the community, which, ironically, provides the most reliable source of self-preservation.

Intellectual credibility weighs on the minds of many people who listen to the sermon through logos settings. Such folk want to know what they can count on and what they cannot. Given the longevity, centrality, and proven record of the virtue of repentance in the Christian community, I thought that while this idea needed explanation, it did not need defense. In connection with discussing integrity in the previous section on ethos settings, I noted an issue that calls for reflection of this kind—the degree to which a community believes that the world is about to come to an apocalyptic end, or the degree to which a community believes in another mode of eschatology. The length of the sermon did not allow a lengthy discussion of different approaches to eschatology, but I did decide to include a mini-comparison and contrast of Luke's apocalyptic eschatology and my own approach to such things since I think the latter is more credible than the former.

Knowing that congregants who synthesize the sermon through logos perspectives are drawn to sermons that help make sense of life, I considered whether this sermon opened the door for such an activity. I suspected that some of the listeners would respond to an issue represented by a line in the text, "Whoever has two coats must share with anyone who has none." The coat, of course, is a multilayered symbol bespeaking not only actual coats, but things that make it possible to live comfortably and without unnecessary anxiety about the future. The shameful truth is that I never think I have quite enough resources to sustain my life, especially as I think about living to old age and possibly facing long-term residence in an expensive senior citizen facility or a financially catastrophic illness. Where do I get the strength to share what I have (and which I am afraid of losing), even for the sake of those who have less?

The worship space was built in the form of an amphitheater, so I knew the congregation could see that I had paper material in front of me and would know that I was prepared. In the content of the sermon itself, however, I also tried to include remarks to indicate that I had done some research and thinking leading up to the sermon.

Appeals to Pathos

People who engage the sermon through the portal of pathos hope for the sermon to inspire them. They are most likely to receive the sermon in a positive way and to act on it when the sermon touches them either by generating feelings that directly provide an emotional experience of the main message of the sermon, or by evoking emotions that, while not directly related to the subject of the message, create an emotional climate that listeners associate positively with the sermon.

As the direction of the sermon became clear, I hoped that it would inspire people to repent. Because feeling is a mode of knowledge for persons who approach the sermon through pathos settings, I hoped the sermon could touch the congregation in the realm of feeling. For congregants whose point of entry into the sermon is pathos, a decision to repent is much more than a rational matter, that is, more than the logical outcome of close theological reasoning centering on theological propositions and arguments. I imagined that for people who attend to the sermon on pathos settings, the desire to repent could be empowered by feelings of sadness and shame over the circumstances that prompt the need for repentance, by emotional identification with persons who will benefit from the sharing that results from repentance (e.g., people who have no coat), and especially by the sense that the future will feel better to them if they repent.

I sought for the sermon to generate feelings that would contribute to the congregation's wanting to repent largely by including evocative material in the sermon that deals directly with the motif of repentance, while hoping that other material in the sermon would help create a listening environment of positive associations with the sermon. I also hoped to avoid setting off feelings that would get in the way of the desire to continue listening to the sermon and to repent.

The text itself provokes emotion in several ways. The emotional setting of the text is one of anxiety arising from economic and social uncertainty. Many were in poverty and in constant search of food, clothing, and shelter. Even those who lived in relative economic security daily faced Roman occupation and its constant threat of repression and violence. I wanted the sermon to help the congregation feel what that world was like, and to recognize points at which feelings are similar in our world.

The text provokes a feeling of discomfort. Luke wants the crowd in the text (and the readers of the gospel) to feel uncomfortable with the fact that the prophet sees them as "a brood of vipers" and with taking false security in the notion that they have Sarah and Abraham as their parents. Luke wants this discomfort to prompt readers to examine themselves with an eye towards what they need to do to become more faithful. I hope that the sermon will create a similar kind of uneasiness in the congregation. To borrow a term from one of the interviewees, I hope that the sermon will contain moments of "squirming" in which listeners consider things that they can do to bring their lives more fully into line with God's purposes (and, thereby, to end the squirming).

The text deftly evokes a feeling of emotional identification with those who have no coats, no food, and who are gouged and threatened. When Luke mentions a person who has no coat, we feel the cold around that person in the winter and the unrelenting sun in the summer. When Luke mentions a person who has no food, I feel a sympathetic hunger pang. When Luke mentions the tax collectors and the soldiers, I feel the frustration that comes from being gouged. And when Luke mentions the soldiers, I feel the fear and hostility that come from being threatened. In the sermon, I wanted to evoke how it felt to have no coat in that world, and to evoke a similar feeling of what it feels to have insufficient resources in the world today in the hope that such a feeling would become a motivation to repent and to share.

The text aims to inspire the related feelings of hope that a new world (the realm of God) is coming and a desire to be a part of that world. Luke does not describe the new world in this passage, but invokes the reader's expectation of it. The text functions as a lure to the reader to turn away from the world of anxiety, hunger, and exploitation and to turn to the divine realm. I suspect that many people in the first century felt a longing for this world. The question, "What then should we do?" functions to name how Luke hopes the congregation will respond to the lure of the new age: The congregation will want to know how to join the movement toward that age. I sought for persons who listen to the sermon through pathos settings to resonate intuitively with this hope. I further hoped that the sermon would help them name this impulse, and that their yearning for a better world would become a source for power for repentance.

The announcement of the imminence of the end of the present age of history through an apocalypse, and judgment resulting in some people being consigned to an "unquenchable fire," generates feelings of fear and of bewilderment. The fear, of course, is that one may be cast into the fire. The urge to avoid such a fate could be a powerful motivation to repentance. At the same time, as I noted in connection with logos settings just above, many people do not believe that the world is headed towards a singular apocalyptic cataclysm, and, hence, feel some confusion around this text. The preacher can help such folk name the source of their feeling of confusion and resolve it by clarifying what today's congregation can believe concerning this judgment.[12] At the same time, I have the impression that some people who listen to the sermon through pathos settings have an intuitive sense that judgment of the kind depicted in this text need not be associated only with a specific moment of apocalypse, but they have a more figurative understanding of judgment as taking place repeatedly in many times and places.

People who tune into the homily through pathos settings are often moved by stories. Some of these folk can even describe the qualities of stories that touch them—the use of descriptive language, a plot that builds, characters that are real (and not out of a sermon illustration book), and language that refers to the senses. One of the hardest tasks that I routinely face in sermon preparation is finding life-like stories for sermons. For the sermon on John's invitation to repentance, I located, primarily from my own memory, some stories that speak of individual acts of repentance. I would like to have included a story about my personal experience that brought repentance to life, however, I could not come up with one that fit this sermon.[13]

I aimed for the emotions with which people responded to the sermon not to become ends in themselves. That may happen when a preacher tells a touching story, especially a story about someone in need or in pain; the experience of the emotion may feel like all the response that some listeners need to make to the sermon, when, in fact, a faithful response calls for further thought or action. I sought to make it clear in the sermon that feelings aroused by the sermon should lead to repentance.

The emotional climate for the preaching of this sermon was complicated by the fact that the former president of Iraq, Saddam Hussein, was captured just a few hours before the service of worship. News about this event filled every television broadcast and every radio station. Members of the congregation who talked about the capture in the hallway before the service exhibited diverse responses ranging from happy to sad. Some felt gleeful.

"We got him." Some were somber as they wondered what Hussein's capture would mean for continuing Iraqi military action. Would this event inspire more resistance to the U.S. occupation, and, hence, more violence and killing? Some who had opposed the invasion of Iraq felt sorry because they feared the capture would become a significant public relations coup for the policy of invasion, and would be used to justify unilateral U.S. military action against other nations. Because emotions around this event were so fresh and strong, I thought I needed to say something about it fairly early in the sermon. As indicated in the reflections on logos settings just above, I was not in a position to give a thoughtful response to the capture, but I hoped that naming it would defuse some of its emotional magnetic field and would free people who listen to the sermon through pathos settings to focus on the themes particular to this sermon.

I hoped to embody the sermon in such a way that my voice and body communicated emotions appropriate to the content of the sermon. I wanted to express the passion and urgency that seems to pulse through John's preaching while avoiding an angry tone for two reasons: (a) I exegetically contend that Luke is not angry but is passionately pleading for the congregation to repent. (b) Some of the interviewees in the study indicate that when a preacher expresses anger towards a congregation, people often diminish in their willingness to continue listening to the sermon. Some parts of the sermon called for a tone of empathy with the suffering felt by persons mentioned in the sermon, such as people in antiquity and today who have no shirt and no food. A few parts of the sermon were rather light-hearted.

The sermon on Luke 3:7–18 follows. Annotations call attention to points at which I attempted to appeal to particular settings. Brief descriptions of how I hoped the listener would receive the sermon follow the various parts of the message. I reproduce the manuscript with much of its oral quality intact (including sentence fragments).

The Sermon

Things about John the Baptist both draw me to him and push me away. "You brood of vipers." Those words leave a bad taste in my mouth. "You are children of the snake that tempted Adam and Eve in the garden." If John was a teenager in our house, and he said that to me, John would be grounded forever.

I hoped the opening paragraph would spark curiosity as to what in the text is both attractive and distancing (a logos concern). I also hoped the congregation would perceive that I am "one of them" (an ethos concern) since I am part of a family that struggles with issues familiar to many of them (the behavior of youths). I projected rightly, judging by the congregation's gentle laughter at the last line, that the beginning would contribute to a positive feeling about the sermon (a pathos phenomenon).

> At the same time, there is an almost visceral attraction to John. "Bear fruits worthy of repentance." Why? Because John knows that the world in which we live is a hard place—sin, injustice, exploitation, violence, death. People who are homeless and hungry. Kids that talk back. The stocks you so carefully set aside for your old age lose value every month. Indiana manufacturing plants close and leave people out of work. In Iraq yesterday, the seventeenth Hoosier was killed. I have not personally been connected to the networks of anyone killed there, but before this war is over, I expect to be. And just a few hours ago, Saddam Hussein was captured.
>
> John believes that God is bringing a new world. A world of forgiveness, justice, community, love, peace, and life. John is in the wilderness to bring a word of hope. Christians, of course, believe that Jesus Christ is God's agent bringing the new age.

I thought the preceding paragraphs would appeal to people who listen to the sermon through logos settings with its clear analogy of similarities between the world of John and our world and to people who listen through pathos settings with emotions evoked by the term "visceral" and by one-phrase and one-sentence images of people in situations of distress. This part of the sermon is also designed to invoke a feeling of hope by calling attention to God's desire to create a new world.

> But between the present world and the new world is a great judgment. "Even now, the axe is lying at the root of the trees; every tree therefore that does not bear good fruit is cut down and thrown into the fire." Run your finger down the blade of the axe. Feel how razor-sharp it is? Can you hear the roar of the flames? Smell the smoke? Feel its heat?

This paragraph and the next explain an aspect of the text (Luke's belief in a great judgment) that is particularly important to people who listen to the sermon on the logos setting and want to know the meaning of the language about the axe, the tree, and the fire. I appeal directly to pathos by inviting the congregation to run their fingers down the blade of the axe and to "feel how razor-sharp it is," and to feel the fire.

> John, of course, is using figures of speech to alert the crowd to the coming of the last great judgment. A moment in life when the evil that people in the world do catches up with them, and they suffer the consequences. Not everyone today, myself included, believe that there will be such a single, dramatic moment of judgment. Nor does everyone today believe in a punishment of unquenchable fire. But buried deep at the center of John's preaching is a conviction that is as true today as when John spoke it: Our attitudes and behaviors bear consequences. If we go along with

dishonesty, injustice, exploitation, violence and death, we can expect our personal lives, and our social worlds to be stained by dishonesty, injustice, exploitation, violence, and death.

Integrity, a trait of particular value to people for whom pathos settings are the incipient mode of processing the sermon, compels me to state a point at which my own theology of judgment takes a different tack from Luke. The sermon is not long enough to allow time for more than simply mentioning it.

The crowds in the wilderness want to avoid this judgment and to live towards the new realm of peace, justice, and love. So do I. When they ask John a question, it is my question, also. And if you have felt the pain of brokenness in this life, and the longing for a better life in a better world, I'll bet it is your question, too. "What then should we do? How do we bear fruit worthy of repentance? How do we repent?"

These questions are intended to be real questions and not simply questions to effect a transition from one part of the sermon to another. These questions are supposed to provoke thought (a characteristic of sermons that motivate people who hear through logos settings to engage the sermon). I anticipated an ethos connection between the congregation and the crowd, and between the congregation and me, when I suggest that the crowd's question could also be the congregation's question.

I used to think of repentance as feeling bad, feeling sorry and remorseful. While repentance in Judaism included feeling sorry, it involved much more. Repentance is the act of turning away from collusion with the old age and of turning towards the new world that God is bringing. Even more, an act of repentance is a sign of commitment to living in God's ways and it is an act of preparation for the new age.

In those days, tax collectors could force people to pay not only the basic tax, but a surcharge that went into the tax collectors' pockets. Soldiers could extort protection money from people by threat or even false accusations. We expect tax collectors to repent by not gouging people and collecting only the amount required. We expect soldiers to repent by not extorting people, threatening them, or falsely accusing them.

But John also gives repentance an unexpected spin. "Whoever has two coats must share with anyone who has none, and whoever has food must do likewise." If you have two coats, giving one to a person who has none can be an act of repentance. How? Coats and food represent things that are necessary for a secure and blessed life. A common human propensity is to stock up stuff to provide for our own security in the future. Luke, however, believes that the new world is coming soon. When you pass along your second coat, you turn away from protecting yourself and turn towards the new world in which God cares for all. You show a sign of trust that this new world is coming and that God will provide for you as you provide for others.

The three paragraphs above explain (a logos preference) the idea of repentance and provide information about repentance and about tax collectors and soldiers. I thought the unexpected spin on repentance would stretch the ways in which the congregation has thought about repentance. I expected that mentioning the tax collectors and soldiers gouging and extorting would prompt an emotional response.

John preached in a time of poverty, financial anxiety, and social stress. Many people felt the chill of having little clothing. Many people felt their stomachs growl with hunger. Many people, living from day to day, put their hands in their pockets, and had no change to rattle.

I try to use language that appeals to the senses and creates feelings (cold, hunger, an empty pocket), thereby stirring pathos.

If *you* have clothing, John says, two coats, repent by giving one to the person who does not have a coat. If *you* have food, repent by giving some food to the hungry. If *you* have sufficient financial resources, John says, repent by not accumulating more than you need and by sharing with those who are in need.

The injunction to share clothing, food, and financial resources to persons who have none appeals to the ethos inclination to reach out. When embodying the sermon, I tried to stress the italicized words in the hope that the vocal emphasis would spark a pathos response.

Think of what such actions would mean to the child who will wait for the bus on a dark corner in the snow and the cold tomorrow morning, wearing only a sweatshirt because there is no coat. Think of what this would mean to the person rummaging in a dumpster behind a nearby restaurant early on a Sunday morning, looking for food.

I hoped that the images of the child waiting in the snow and the person rummaging in the dumpster would serve as a lure to repentance, especially through the pathos stirred by feelings of being cold and hungry.

Repentance is one of the fundamental themes of Advent. How do we prepare for Christmas? By turning away from the things that deny blessing to ourselves and others, and by taking the positive, dynamic action of turning toward things that create abundance and justice for all.

Now a remarkable thing is that repentance works two ways. It helps other people and it helps you. It helps other people by making the world more like the place God wants it to be. It helps you by releasing you from fear and self-centeredness, and grasping after stuff that you hope will make you secure, only to realize you will never have enough.

Again, a clear explanation of how repentance works is aimed at providing logos, information.

> There is a catch, of course, and I feel it myself. Not knowing what tomorrow will bring, how do you know you won't need your second coat? Your food? Your money? It's *so* hard. But here is where the Episcopal Church points a way forward in the form of the collect for the day, the one that begins, "Stir up your power, O God." This prayer is a source of considerable humor among other Christians because the first words "Stir up" sound like a part of a saddle on a horse. I'm a little surprised, in fact, that your pastor did not instruct me to wear a cowboy hat. (Of course, then you might have mistaken me for the bishop.)
>
> > Stir up your power, O God, and with great might come among us, and because we are sorely hindered by our sins, let your bountiful grace and mercy speedily help and deliver us.[14]
>
> We can repent not because *we* make ourselves repent, but because God's power and grace are among us. Such a great God: *giving* us the very thing we need to do what we need to do.

I thought that turning to a resource that is recognized as an authority in the congregation would encourage positive ethos while also communicating a significant theological idea (a logos quality). I hoped that the reference to the cowboy hat and the bishopric would create a light moment and its indirect self-deprecation would reinforce the sense that I was "one of the people." As I preached, however, I thought that these comments (especially about the bishopric) broke the mood of the sermon and distracted the listeners.

> Now if we had time this morning, we could follow Luke's story into the book of Acts where we would learn that in the early church, God provides for all by means of sharing in the community. That's the point of that famous phrase, "had all things in common" (Acts 2:44). If I give up my second coat, and then find next year, that the one I kept has worn out, the community will provide another. Instead of trying to hoard for my own security all by myself, the life of the community is our security.

The strong affirmation of the working of God's power in the midst of the community (logos) in the collect was intended to be an antidote to the hesitation and even fear (pathos) of repenting through sharing. I had similar hopes that the reference to providence mediated through sharing by the early church in the Acts would function similarly.

> One of the wonderful things about this time of year is that there are so many opportunities to express John's kind of repentance. Some things simple and easy to do—like the Salvation Army kettles, or bringing food

for the families the congregation is sponsoring, or adding to the Angel Tree, or returning your House-shaped Box filled with money. And with a little more effort, you can donate a pint of blood, or take a turn working at Gleaners Food Bank or at the Dayspring Shelter.

Simple, yes. To be sure, such things can be little more than donations to charity. But if we act from Luke's perspective on repentance, then turning over some of our money, time, and blood can be the first step turning away from hanging on to our own lives, and turning towards the divine realm with its better life for all. Indeed, something as ordinary as putting money in the Salvation Army kettle can become a pattern for things we do all year. If you can turn over a little bit to the good of the community now, you can make it a way of life.

As mentioned above, I tried to illustrate specific repentant actions the congregation could take. Several of the items in this list (e.g., the Angel Tree, the House-shaped Boxes) refer to congregational projects. Such references appeal especially (though not exclusively) to persons who hear the sermon on ethos settings and who want to know how the sermon relates to the particular world in which they live.

Some things are more complicated and require a bigger stretch and more imagination. If God does not want financial security to float with the value of stocks rising and falling like the temperature in Indiana at this time of the year, or to see manufacturing plants closing across town, we can turn away from thinking that such events are just the way things are, and ask the question, "What can we do to help develop a world economy in which there are good jobs for all?" I do not myself have the details of a plan for a way towards greater peace in Iraq, but I can join groups, such as "Move On" who call into question the idea that we should just assume that the killing will go on and who are looking at alternatives. From John's point of view, these things are acts of repentance that help prepare us for the coming of Christ, and for the new world of abundance for all that Christ wants for all.

I try to help the congregation recognize that repentance is more than individual responses to people in need but also involves systemic change. Nevertheless, systemic change does call for individual action.

Repentance does not have to be a big, dramatic act. Not long ago, I visited an upper-middle-class congregation located downtown in a conservative part of southern California. Their minister humorously called them First Church of the Hard Line. Beautiful old Mission-style building with polished brass, carved wood and stained glass that comes alive in the sunlight. Wednesday night dinners followed by a youth program and classes for adults. One night a couple of scruffy looking grade-school-age Hispanic children looked in the open door while they were eating and wandered in.

Kids looking longingly at food. What do you do? The kids came back and gradually their story came out. They had come from Mexico, had been abandoned by their father, and now lived with their four siblings and single-parenting mother, who had a minimum wage job and no prospects of getting a better one because they were in this country illegally. Someone from the congregation took some clothes to the home. They didn't have much food, clothing, or school supplies because so much of their money went to the rent. The mother said if they went back to their part of Mexico, prospects weren't any better. Tedious low-paying work. Poor schools. Limited futures. At least here they had the long-term possibility of working for a better life.

The congregation talked informally about what to do. Report them for deportation? Hard lines are hard to hold when people have names and faces and stories and hearts. You know how these things happen—a bag of clothing turns into a box of food every week and trips to the optometrist and summer camp, and help with school. It also turned into legal advice, and to several members of the congregation coming to think that there are inconsistencies and inequities in U.S. policies regarding persons who are in this country in situations similar to that of the kids who looked in the door of the church that night, and writing letters to Washington to point out these things.

It's not a whole new world. But it's a step away from hanging onto what we've got and a step towards a better one. The minister, a friend of mine, says, "I don't know whether it's the kids or not, but we laugh more now than we used to."

I told this story to appeal to listeners on all three settings. I thought the relationships between the congregation and the household would be an ethos connection, the story would illustrate repentance in a logos way, and the situation of the family (and the congregation's response) would evoke pathos.

From across the centuries, John the Baptist puts a question to us. If we have two coats, what do we need to do?

I hope that the last question will provoke the congregation to continue thinking about the message after the sermon ends.

Epilogue

Several of the listeners in the study point us to an occurrence in listening communities that is familiar (if somewhat frustrating) to many preachers: different people in the same worship service can come away from the sermon with different messages. No matter how carefully a preacher incorporates material in the sermon that incorporates perspectives from this book and other resources for preaching, some people in the congregation will not really hear the sermon that the minister preaches. The listeners in the study offer liberating perspectives within which to view this phenomenon.

An interviewee points out that personal disposition and life circumstance often influences what people take away from the sermon. Near the end of an interview, an interviewer says to an interviewee, "You must be a careful listener."

> I think if the preachers hit me on the right Sunday, I think I'm a pretty good listener. It's not always necessarily the pastor. It's the kind of week you had, what you're reflecting on in your life as you sit in the pew. Sometimes the sermon can touch that part of your life. Other times you're still worrying about it while you're sitting there on a Sunday morning. It could be a variety of things way beyond the pastor's control that the listener is just not going to hear that Sunday.

Another listener points out that even when people arrive at worship relatively refreshed and free of worry:

> There are so many things that interplay–different personalities of people and how people receive messages, and people's different

experiences and spiritual baggage they carry with them. We all respond differently. Everybody in a congregation of a hundred people listening to the sermon, you can have a hundred different interpretations of what's being said in terms of how that applies to one another. Just because a person says a certain thing doesn't necessarily mean I receive it in the way that it's intended to be received.

These listeners call attention to an important factor in preaching: listeners do hear the sermon in the context of their own particularity.

Other interviewees see the differences in what people take away from the sermon as related to divine providence and the work of the Holy Spirit. A member of a congregation in the study is asked, "What do you think God is doing during the sermon?"

If it's a hundred people, and people are going to think different things, maybe twenty of them take one thing away, and five of them take another thing away, and one of them will take something else away. Just the nature of human listening is such that people are not going to hear all of the message anyway. Something is going to strike them, and they're going to start thinking about that a little bit, and they're going to miss the next two points. That's just the nature of listening. What I hope God is doing is providing guidance to whatever point sends them off in their own life thinking about that point that they really needed to hear...What I think God is doing is providing a way for each individual in the congregation to hear the message.

According to this listener's nascent theology of preaching, the preacher can only develop one sermon for the whole congregation, as if "one sizes fits all" when people are really at different listening sizes (so to speak). But in the hearing, God tailors the sermon to each size and thereby provides "guidance for everybody hearing."

Another listener speaks of a similar interpretive work, but in the language of the Holy Spirit.

My experience is that we hear things differently, and that's why God's word is so alive, because what I need to hear and what they need to hear is different, but it comes from the same sermon, which is the Holy Spirit's job. That's what the Spirit does through the whole thing is guiding the minister and helping us interpret.

This listener describes the Spirit's work in bringing diverse responses from one sermon as a great blessing.

These observations underscore an important point made in the early part of the book. No amount of rhetorical finesse can give the preacher control over what happens in the mind, heart, and will of the congregation. The kinds of discoveries that are in this volume concerning ethos, logos, and pathos can only help preachers recognize the kinds of sermons that have a reasonable likelihood of being received in the ways the preacher intends. As one listener says:

> I don't think the preacher can always connect with everybody, but I think you can always structure what you're trying to say to try to capture a larger percentage than a smaller percentage…You have to structure it so that most people can get something of what you're saying.

In the end, the sermon refracts through the experience of the hearer. The Spirit, of course, is always at work in the experience the hearer. The preacher must hope that as listeners pick up on certain aspects of the sermon, bypass others, and make connections that the preacher never had in mind, they will do so in ways that give the Spirit optimum opportunity to work with them.

The Sermon Helps People Make Connections

Throughout this book, I have tried to stay close to the actual words of the people interviewed. It seems fitting, therefore, to end with a voice from the study who affirms the importance of preaching.

> I think that preachers are instructors like I'm an instructor. They're trying to help people see connections. They're trying to help people feel connected, to have a relationship to God and to Jesus. I would assume they're also working to create some feeling of community in the church…I hope that the preacher will help me make sense of the readings for the day, of the gospel. That the person will somehow make me feel more connected to God–remind me of things that I often don't think about in a busy life with lots of competing demands. That somehow I'll feel inspired afterward, either inspired to change the way I think or the way I act or to reflect more on things that I don't think about very often. I hope for inspiration.

We hope this study will help preachers develop sermons that are, in the best sense, inspirational.

Questions Asked in the Interviews

This appendix lists the questions in the study that the interviewers asked 263 laypeople who listen to sermons, according to the categories of ethos, logos, pathos, and embodiment.[1] They are reproduced here because reference is made to them in this book when a particular question or questions provide a context for understanding an interviewee's statement.

Permission is hereby granted to reprint these questions for use in congregations or educational settings.

Questions on Ethos[2]

1. Tell me about how you became a part of this congregation.
2. What are the most important things that happen in this congregation?
3. Describe a typical Sunday morning in this congregation.
4. Tell me what preaching does in this congregation that other things do not do.
5. What would be missing if there were no sermon?
6. Tell me about how preaching shapes your congregation–who you are as a community.
7. Tell me about your history as a person listening to sermons. What are high points? What are some low points? Was there ever a time when you almost walked out?
8. Talk a little bit about your relationship with the pastors and preachers that you have had.
9. Tell me about a pastor you have had who was also a good preacher. What did you like about that person?

Questions on Logos

1. What do you think your pastor is doing when she or he preaches?
2. Tell me about a sermon that you really found engaging.
3. What was it about that sermon that engaged you?
4. Tell me about a sermon that did not interest you. That left you cold?
5. What was it about that sermon that left you cold or put you off?
6. What role does/should the Bible have in preaching?
7. When does a sermon have authority for you?

8. What do you most want to know about God when you hear a sermon?
9. What do you think God is doing during the sermon itself?
10. I'll bet you have heard a sermon that caused you to think or act differently, maybe about some big issue, maybe about a smaller issue. Would you tell me about that sermon?
11. What did the pastor say or do that prompted you to act differently?

Questions on Pathos

1. When the pastor stands up to preach, what do you hope will happen to you as a result of listening to that sermon?
2. I'm going to ask you a question about you personally and then a similar question about the congregation. Can you tell me about a sermon that stirred your own emotions?
3. What in the sermon stirred you?
4. I would like for you to describe a sermon that seemed to move the congregation as a whole, as a community.
5. What was it about that sermon that seemed to move the congregation?
6. Would you describe a time when the sermon stirred emotions that made you feel uncomfortable?
7. When the sermon stirs the emotions of the congregation, what happens after worship?
8. Do you think there are some issues that are just too explosive, too dangerous, for the preacher to deal with in the pulpit? Would you name some of them for me and tell me why you think they are dangerous?

Questions on Embodiment

1. Would you please describe for me a preacher whose physical presence in the pulpit was really good—whose delivery was really engaging?
2. What are some physical things a preacher does (while delivering the sermon) that help you to want to pay attention?
3. Can you think of a time when you could not hear or see the preacher well? How did that affect you?
4. What difference does it make to you when you can see the facial features of the preacher and hear distinctly?

Wanting for the interviewees to have an opportunity to comment on aspects of preaching not prompted by the previous questions, each interview concluded with this particularly open-ended question:

If you had one or two things you could tell preachers that would help them energize you when you are listening to a sermon, what would they be?

This last question often brought forth remarks that were especially pungent and revealing.

Table Comparing Three Settings of Listening

Table 2 offers an abbreviated comparison of how persons on the three different settings listen to selected aspects of preaching. Most of the aspects of preaching that are compared are drawn from the questions asked in the study (listed in appendix A). Other aspects arise from the interviews themselves. In chapters 1–4, I did not discuss every aspect of preaching that appears on this table because the transcripts did not provide extensive discussion of some of these topics or because including them in full-bodied discussions in the previous chapters would have made the book incredibly large and expensive. Some of the material overlaps from one category to another.

Few persons conform in every way to the description of the settings offered here. Indeed, the plural term "settings" is intended to denote variation from person to person. All listeners in the study manifest some characteristics from each setting; as noted in chapters 2–4, a particular listener typically refracts some of the qualities of the other two settings through that person's dominant setting. Listeners are enormously complex and seldom make comments in the interviews that are altogether true to one category.

Congregational culture, though discussed in chapter 2 in relationship to ethos, is not listed as a separate category in this table because it is assumed that all qualities are specific to particular congregations and their distinctive cultures. Embodiment is not discussed as a category in the table because, as we noted in chapter 1, listeners in all three categories identify similar traits in embodiment that engage and disengage them. In chapter 4, we call attention to the distinctive quality of embodiment mentioned by persons who listen on pathos settings.

TABLE 2

Comparison of Leading Characteristics of the Three Settings

	CHARACTERISTICS OF ETHOS SETTINGS	CHARACTERISTICS OF LOGOS SETTINGS	CHARACTERISTICS OF PATHOS SETTINGS
General perspective of this setting	Character of preacher and sense of relationship with preacher and congregation.	Content of the sermon, especially information and ideas that help make sense of life.	Degree to which sermons generate feeling.
Specific qualities of this setting	Want to perceive the preacher as real; seek integrity in preacher; sense of relationship with preacher enhances listening; perceive sermon itself as relationship with preacher; respond to appeals to reach out to (relate with) people beyond congregation.	Content of sermon is focal point of worship; seek information and ideas about Bible, theology, church, and world; ideas *qua* ideas have significant effects on these listeners; want sermon to have orderly structure and make a point; appreciate comparison and contrast of different viewpoints; must see preacher is prepared.	Feeling not simply ephemeral emotion but mode of intuitive knowledge; seek sermons that touch this mode of knowledge (sermons that inspire, move, stir); stirred by stories that evoke feeling, vivid language, personal material from life of preacher with emotional component; sees God moving through feeling; appropriate emotion in embodiment moves listener.
How these settings interact with qualities associated with the other two settings	*Logos* (content of sermon): helpful as interprets relationship with God, with other people and with world. *Pathos*: important as feelings deepen listener's perception of relation with God, preachers, others.	*Ethos*: message more important than messenger; relationship as means to understanding (logos). *Pathos*: moves people to be favorably disposed toward ideas at center of sermon; not very aware of (may even be distrustful of) feeling; feeling prompts reflection; ideas generate feeling.	*Ethos*: concerned about feelings generated by perception of character of preacher and relationships with others; relationship important as expression of feeling. *Logos*: presence of feeling alerts listener to thought; seeks for sermons to interpret feelings; being touched helps remember.
Most important qualities in perception of preacher	Want to perceive that preacher has integrity, is relational.	Want to perceive that preacher is excellent thinker who brings forth intellectually stimulating ideas.	Want to perceive that preacher has deep feelings, and cares about congregation and subject of sermon.
View of the purpose of preaching	Perception of character of (and relationship with) pastor models relationship of members of congregation with one another; sermon interprets relationships.	Preaching offers stimulating ideas and information that interpret meaning of life.	Preaching helps people feel closer to God and one another by stirring emotions; helps listeners interpret feelings; speaks to listener at level of feeling—adds to knowledge at level of feeling.

High points in history of listening	When preacher had exemplary character; when listener had close relationship with preacher.	Sermons that put forth challenging ideas.	When deeply touched (even moved to tears).
How stories function	Stories demonstrate character of preacher; model relationships and warn against destructive qualities in relationships.	Stories illustrate points.	Stories evoke feeling; contribute to realm of feeling knowledge.
How preaching shapes congregation	Preaching shapes congregation through listener's perception of experiencing relationship with preacher, and by preacher talking about relationships and about how people connect with one another; help people locate opportunities to reach out.	Preaching shapes congregation by imparting information and ideas; ideas have formative power.	Preaching shapes congregation by creating reservoir of shared feelings; congregation develops a common emotional history.
View of the role of Bible	Bible helps community determine faithful, trustworthy character, as well as faithful relationships.	Bible is full of information and ideas that congregation needs to know about, evaluate, and apply.	Bible is record of how people in past have felt in response to God, one another, and how people today can do so; encounters with Bible stir feeling (awe, love, fear, etc.).
Authority of the sermon	Character of the preacher is key; sermon has authority when these listeners trust preacher and have sense of being in positive relationship with preacher.	Sermon is authoritative when contains ideas and information that these listeners believe are true.	Sermon is authoritative when it touches people in positive way; many of these listeners speak of simply "knowing" (i.e. through feeling) that sermon is true.
What do you most want to know about God?	How God relates with congregation, world; how community can have positive relationship with God.	What these listeners can believe about God. What is true? What can we count on?	These listeners want to have positive feeling about God; also want to deal with feelings of fear, guilt, judgment prompted by Bible and types of preaching that emphasize those traits.
Factors that prompt different thinking or acting	These listeners change in order to accommodate requirements of relationships with God, preacher, congregation, and world.	These listeners change when they come to think (through logic, evidence, and argument) that a certain perspective or behavior makes more logical sense than another.	These listeners think or act differently in response to feeling: they change in order to feel better or to avoid pain, and to help other people feel better and other people avoid pain.

Typical Expressions Associated with Each Setting

The language a person uses often signals that person's orientation to the sermon. Persons who enter the sermon on each different setting frequently use words that are associated with that setting. For example, a congregant with a logos predisposition often says, "I think," and talks about ideas and concepts. People for whom an experience of pathos is usually necessary for them to feel fully engaged often speak in the vocabulary of "feeling."[3]

Here are some expressions that are typically associated with the three settings.[4] These words, phrases, and sentences are either quoted or adapted from the interviews. I repeat that an interpreter cannot simply take the presence of one of these remarks as a signal that a person enters the sermon on the setting with which the remark is associated here. These words, phrases, and sentences, and others that tend to be associated with specific settings, need to be interpreted in the context of the whole interview so as to get a sense of how the settings interact for that person. But when they occur repeatedly in a person's comments on preaching, they often signal that person's base listening setting

Ethos	
I relate with the pastor	The sermon connects with me
The sermon unifies congregation	Preaching brings people together
The preacher knows my life	Preacher is anointed person
I identify with the preacher	Preacher needs to walk the walk
The sermon draws every one in	Emphasis on caring for one another
The preacher walks where I walk	Homily bonds congregation toward a goal
The message enhances the community	The sermons seem so sincere

Preacher is ambassador for God	Sermons help us connect globally
What comes across to me is being able to relate to the person doing the preaching	I tune out when pastor does not appear to be talking with anyone in the congregation
The sermon enhances the community of the church	The sermon is more meaningful when I know the preacher on a personal level
A sermon has authority because pastor preaches it	Repeated emphasis on preacher being warm, personable outside the pulpit
The preacher connected with me because she took a big risk...and bared her weaknesses and struggles	Emphasis in interview on members of congregation caring for one another

Logos

I think	The sermon teaches
Make the point	I am hoping I will learn more
I want to know	The sermon should be clear
I want the sermon to apply to life	We want a better understanding
Quit when you've made your point	The sermon is too complicated
Sermons needs to clarify issues	I want the sermon to challenge me to think
I listen for new ideas	Preacher needs to tell the truth
I need a message that makes sense	I need the pastor to interpret
The sermon gives me something to ponder	The sermon helps me consider
I like for the preacher to examine	The homily helps me conceive a new way
We want the preacher to convince us	I want to know what the preacher believes
Sermon should be well thought out	The pastor stimulates me intellectually
I come to church for the message	Sermons lead you to reflect on
I want the sermon to give me a new slant	I seek new information from the sermon
We need real meat	This preacher has such insight
I like for the sermon to expose options then let me decide	Preaching helps people change their and minds

Pathos

I feel	The preacher speaks through her heart
The sermon touches me	The sermon moves me
I am stirred	I listen for inspiration
The message lifts me right up	People come to be filled
Some sermons leave me cold	Preaching convicts me
Speaker is passionate	I feel a quickening during the sermon
My emotions are stirred	The emotional hook really gets me
I feel this fullness	I feel it in my heart
Sermon fails when Pastor does not feel it	The sermon is so sensitive
The message excites me	The preacher has such fire
If you're trying to offer intellectual comfort when someone is hurting in the congregation, you're not going to connect	

Notes

Introduction

[1]The names of these parishioners are fictional.

[2]This perspective is based on an empirical study of people who listen to sermons described more fully in chapter 1. Although this particular book is written by one person who must take responsibility for its content, it reflects the work of a team of scholars who worked together in the study "Listening to Listeners," funded by the Lilly Endowment and carried out through Christian Theological Seminary in Indianapolis, Ind., USA: Ronald J. Allen, Dale P. Andrews, Jon L. Berquist, L. Susan Bond, John S. McClure, Dan P. Moseley, Mary Alice Mulligan, G. Lee Ramsey, Jr., Diane Turner-Sharazz, and Dawn Ottoni Wilhelm.

[3]The study itself investigated four qualities (ethos, logos, pathos, and embodiment), but this book discusses only ethos, logos, and pathos because we did not find any listeners for whom embodiment was the main setting through which they interact with the sermon.

[4]While this book makes use of these categories to help explain how people listen to sermons, it also modifies them as explained in later chapters.

[5]For further discussion of the designation "settings," see chapter 1, footnote 11. The team who worked on the research project on which this book is based has not been able to find a single term that brings together the oral-aural-visual qualities of the event of preaching in a way that comprehensively captures the complex dynamics at work in a congregant in the interaction of the category that functions as the major setting of the self with the other two categories. The preacher needs to remember that the human being is a living organism that is more dynamic and nuanced than the amplification mechanism of a sound system. To guard against a possible misuse of the analogy of the settings of a sound system and the settings through which a listener hears a sermon, I state emphatically that the purpose of the study and of this book is not to give preachers tools by which to control what listeners hear, think, and do. Preachers do not (and cannot) control these settings. The purpose of this book is to help preachers understand how many congregants respond to sermons so that preachers can shape messages in accord with the ways in which people actually listen and, hence, enhance communication between the pulpit and the pew.

[6]In a mixing console, the settings would mix such things as the treble and bass qualities in the sound. The mixing can greatly change the listener's perception of the preacher's voice.

[7]This figure was suggested by John S. McClure and was created by Joyce Krauser, Faculty Administrator at Christian Theological Seminary.

[8]For example, nearly every minister has the experience of preaching a sermon that, by all accounts, should be a dud, yet a parishioner will effuse that it was one of the best sermons that the preacher has ever spoken. Something in the sermon connected with the listener in ways that the preacher did not expect but that proved very meaningful for the listener.

Chapter 1: Three Settings through Which People Hear Sermons

[1]I discussed the findings of this book with a minister who said, "Oh, no. Not another typology of how people think." Readers who are familiar with other ways of interpreting how people process thoughts, feelings, and actions will recognize some similarities between the typology suggested in this book and some other typologies. For example, another book with which I was involved explores preaching and different modes of mental process in faith development theory, the Myers-Briggs Type Indicator, Neuro-Linguistic Programming, and women's ways of knowing. See Joseph R. Jeter, Jr. and Ronald J. Allen, *One Gospel, Many Ears: Preaching for Different Listeners in the Congregation* (St. Louis: Chalice Press, 2002), 49–92. Another pattern of interpretation in popular use is Howard Gardner, *Frames of Mind: The Theory of Multiple Intelligences* (New York: Basic Books, 1983) and idem, *Multiple Intelligences: The Theory in Practice* (New York: Basic Books, 1993). Recently scholars in the field of preaching have begun giving more attention to patterns of listening and interpretation associated with different cultures, e.g., James R. Neiman and Thomas G. Rogers, *Preaching to Every Pew: Cross Cultural Strategies* (Philadelphia: Fortress Press, 2001). Some characteristics of ethos, logos, and pathos settings echo themes in other typologies of awareness and communication. However, this book and other approaches do not simply overlap. While there are differences and distinctions

between the approach presented in this volume and others, the purpose of this book is not to sort them out. The fact of so many different ways of understanding human thought, feeling, action, relationship, orientation to the world, and communication points to the fact that these are immensely complex and multilayered matters. No one psychology, sociology, or approach to communication can account for the full range of human awareness and interaction. An author or school of thought can only hope to help illuminate limited aspects of such thick and rich processes.

[2]The data from the study does not provide material to answer the question, "*Why* do people tend to enter the sermon on one of these three settings?" Is it a matter of socialization in the home or by virtue of hearing a certain kind of preaching? Is the cause physiological? Are other reasons in play? More work is needed along these lines.

[3]The data from the study does not provide longitudinal perspectives that allow us to know for sure that people do (or do not) change settings over time. It is reasonable to suppose that the settings are not intractable, but that, from time to time, the settings on a person's control panel may change in response to changes in personal life circumstances, changes in the congregation, or developments in the larger world.

[4]For a survey of previous attempts to take account of how listeners hear sermons, see Ronald J. Allen, "The Turn Toward the Listener: A Selective Review of a Recent Trend in Preaching," *Encounter* 64 (2003): 167–96.

[5]The project is described more fully in John S. McClure, Ronald J. Allen, Dale P. Andrews, L. Susan Bond, Dan P. Moseley, and G. Lee Ramsey, Jr., *Listening to Listeners: Homiletical Case Studies* (St. Louis: Chalice Press, 2004) that contains (and discusses) the transcripts of six full-length interviews from the study. The excerpts from the transcripts that are discussed in the present book were taken from interviews similar to the ones reported in *Listening to Listeners.*

[6]We spoke with 128 in individual interviews and the remainder of the 263 interviewees in small group interviews. Sixteen of the congregations are mainly made up of persons who are non-Hispanic European , nine congregations are primarily African American, and three congregations are racially mixed. The churches come from the long-established denominations and are located in rural, small town, suburban, and urban settings. They include congregations of various sizes–small, medium, large, mega church. The interviews lasted about an hour each. Each interview was tape recorded and transcribed. Writing this book, I worked from transcriptions of the interviews of individuals. The congregations in the study are from the following denominations and Christian movements: African Methodist Episcopal Church, African Methodist Episcopal Zion Church, American Baptist Church, Christian Church (Disciples of Christ), Christian Churches and Churches of Christ, Church of the Brethren, Episcopal Church, Evangelical Lutheran Church in America, Mennonite Church, National Baptist Church, non-denominational community churches, Presbyterian Church in the U.S.A., and United Methodist Church.

[7]On these qualities see Aristotle, *The "Art" of Rhetoric,* tr. John Henry Freese, Loeb Classical Library 23 (Cambridge: Harvard University Press, 1932), 17 (1.2.4–6). For contemporary discussions see Lucy Lind Hogan and Robert Reid, *Connecting with the Congregation: Rhetoric and the Art of Preaching* (Nashville: Abingdon Press, 1999) as well as David S. Cunningham, *Faithful Persuasion: In Aid of a Rhetoric of Christian Theology* (Notre Dame, Ind.: University of Notre Dame Press, 1990).

[8]As indicated elsewhere, we did not find that embodiment functions as a "setting" in the same way as ethos, logos, and pathos.

[9]For samples of the transcripts annotated to demonstrate the principles of interpretation that were applied to each transcript in the study, as well as guidance for conducting interviews in one's own congregation, see McClure et al., *Listening to Listeners,* 21–124.

[10]I try to maintain a helpful balance between citing the words of the interviewees themselves and offering interpretive comments. On the one hand, I hope the book is more than a string of quotes from the interviews. On the other hand, I hope not to obscure the actual words of the persons interviewed with my commentary and interpretation. I hope that readers can hear the listeners speak for themselves.

[11]The project team faced a major (and continuing) challenge in finding adequate vocabulary with which to speak about the listeners and their relationship to the settings. When we began to work with the notion that people begin listening to the sermon on one

setting, we spoke of "the ethos listener," "the logos listener," and "the pathos listener." These singular expressions have the advantages of identifying the primary setting on which the listener receives the sermon and of being compact and easy to use. However, these terms began to sound too reductionistic, as if a person whom we called "an ethos listener" heard the sermon only on the ethos setting.

While it was an easy decision not to speak of a person as "an ethos listener," it is much more difficult to find terminology that is economical, expressive, and that suggests something of the complexity of listening. Based on the analogy of the act of listening to a sermon as similar to being in a sanctuary in which the environment for listening is determined (to a certain degree) by the settings on sound system, we decided to speak in terms of the setting through which a person hears the sermon. One setting functions as the medium through which a listener synthesizes the other settings. We sometimes speak of a person "beginning to listen" through one setting or of a setting being a "port (or point of) entry into the sermon." This language suggests that while the listener typically begins to listen through one setting, other settings (and the mix of settings) affect the ways the hearer responds to the appeals of the sermon. The first setting is a kind of electrical field within which other settings operate while suggesting that other settings simultaneously exert force and alter the primary field.

Similar turns of phrase that appear in this book include (with numerous permutations) "setting through which the listener begins to synthesize the message," "begins to process the sermon," "channel on which the person hears the sermon," "person who listens through [one of the settings]," "portal through which the parishioner engages the sermon," "initial mode of hearing the message," "band through which the congregant is affected by preaching," "tune into the homily," "usually begins to receive the sermon through [one of the settings]," "orientation to listening," "setting through which the listener synthesizes other settings," "primary setting," "incipient quality of listening."

While the revised terminology of "settings" is an improvement over our initial efforts to speak of "the ethos listener" (and cognates), the newer vocabulary is not completely satisfactory. The formulations that speak of "beginning" to process the sermon or the "initial" point of entry could be misinterpreted to mean that the listener first (in time) hears the primary setting of the sermon and only later begins to meld the other settings into the listening gestalt. We do not mean to imply such a temporal, sequential process since multiple settings are frequently at work in the self at the same time.

[12]We found these patterns to be across the various cohorts of the study: women and men, African Americans and persons of non-Hispanic European origin, different ages, different sizes and locations of congregations, the various denominations or movements, etc.

[13]An analyst cannot determine the setting through which the listener processes the sermon on the basis of a single response in a transcript but must find clues running through the interview. A listener can respond to questions in ways that are almost purely associated with that question and without indicating the overarching perspective through which that person processes the sermon. A person who begins to receive the sermon through the logos setting, for instance, can respond to ethos questions with direct ethos responses. A researcher must always interpret individual listener responses in the context of the whole interview.

[14]We can often become aware of a pattern by paying attention to the language that the interviewee uses, for people often use language that is characteristics of their primary setting. We list some examples of language associated with each setting in appendix A.

[15]We are often asked, "What percentage of people tune into the sermon through each setting?" We spoke with 128 people in individual interviews and 135 in small group settings. The individual interviews provide enough data from each person to come to a fairly confident conclusion about each person's setting for listening to a sermon. The number of remarks by each individual in the small group interviews is far fewer, and seldom provides enough depth or breadth to ascertain a person's listening orientation. While we think the individual interviews constitute a large enough number to come to the general conclusions voiced in this study, the number of persons interviewed (in relationship with the fact that the selection of persons to be interviewed was not sufficiently random) does not furnish a large enough or random enough body of data from which to answer the question above. In the sample in the study population, distributions among ethos, logos, and pathos are about the same in African Americans and listeners of non-Hispanic European origin, as well as among women and men, and across the various age cohorts and denominations represented in the study. We

would be especially hesitant to make generalizations regarding the broader African American listening community since the African American population in the interviews was drawn largely from churches whose theological worlds, and liturgical traditions, at least in earlier years, were often associated with those historic Western denominations—Episcopal, African Methodist Episcopal, African Methodist Episcopal Zion. We did not interview in large numbers of African American Baptist, independent, charismatic, or Pentecostal churches.

[16]Such listeners typically leave clues elsewhere in the interview that emotion does play a role in their response to sermons, but usually it is not as prominent a role as logos.

[17]We initially tried to graph the interaction of the various settings in a listener using a pie chart. While the pie chart showed proportions of the listening settings, it did not show the point of entry or interactions among the various settings. We derived the notion of a concept tree from Will C. van den Hoonaard, *Working with Sensitizing Concepts: Analytical Field Research,* A Sage University Paper (Thousand Oaks, Calif.: Sage Publications, 1997), esp.37–45. A concept tree is a diagram using the general shape of a tree to show the relationship of various concepts that emerge in the course of research. We actually drew trees in this spirit with the trunk representing the primary mode of listening, and clusters of branches bespeaking the other aspects of listening in relationship to the trunk and one another. This approach, while helpful, seemed too complex and time consuming. We tried interlocking circles in which a large circle represented the primary setting, with smaller circles within the large one depicting the other settings; often the smaller circles overlapped to show interplay among the different aspects of hearing a sermon. However, that approach seemed to suggest that the setting represented by the large circle creates such a field of force that the other settings operate only within it. In fact, the other settings sometimes influence the one through which the listener initially processes the sermon, and sometimes function independently of it.

[18]Andrews' graph proposal has the disadvantage of not representing visually the interaction among the different settings. A three-dimensional graph would be necessary for that purpose.

[19]Although we did not find any listeners for whom embodiment is the primary setting through which they enter the sermon, listeners from all settings reflected on the degree of importance that they attach to embodiment.

[20]The listener is referring to occasions when the minister brings two chairs into the chancel and, for the sermon, has a dialogue with a parishioner. The minister interviews the parishioner about an important aspect of spiritual life, and the minister adds commentary along the way.

[21]This correlation is examined in chapter 4 in connection with pathos.

[22]Such differences are sometimes associated with congregational culture (discussed on 20–21), and sometimes with particular context. One interviewee notes that preachers need to adjust their styles of speaking to the congregation and the context. "You're not going to jump up and down to make a point in a more formal situation, whereas in a campground situation, it could be different."

[23]Several preachers of non-Hispanic European origin with whom I have discussed this study have assumed that most African Americans hear the sermon through the pathos setting and prefer animated embodiment. However, we find in our study group that percentages of African American listeners who incline towards ethos, logos, and pathos are about the same as persons of non-Hispanic European origin. It is true that a greater percentage of African Americans in our study comment on their preferences for a more exuberant embodiment than do listeners of non-Hispanic European origin, but this preference is found among African Americans who enter the sermon through all three settings. Several African Americans who were interviewed expressed predilections for quieter modes of preaching. We recognize the narrow range of congregations and denominations in our study sample. A different sample might yield different findings. Diversity, it seems, is a characteristic of all listening cohorts.

[24]About 100 people attended the conference, about a third of whom had been interviewed for the project. The others were mainly pastors, with a few laity, from the project area.

Chapter 2: Ethos Settings

[1]Aristotle, *the "Art" of Rhetoric,* tr. John Henry Freese, Loeb Classical Library 23 (Cambridge: Harvard University Press, 1932), 17 (1.2.4).

²Lucy Lind Hogan and Robert Reid, *Connecting with the Congregation: Rhetoric and the Art of Preaching* (Nashville: Abingdon Press, 1999), 50–65.

³David S. Cunningham, *Faithful Persuasion: In Aid of a Rhetoric of Christian Theology* (Notre Dame, Ind.: University of Notre Dame Press, 1990), 132–39.

⁴Lind Hogan and Reid, *Connecting with the Congregation,* 53–60.

⁵Cunningham, *Faithful Persuasion,* 127–31, 139–47.

⁶For guides that discuss more broadly the discipline of congregational studies, see John S. McClure, et al., *Listening to Listeners: Homiletical Case Studies* (St. Louis: Chalice Press, 2004), 149–164 as well as Don M. Wardlaw, "Preaching as the Interface of Two Social Worlds: The Congregation as Corporate Agent in the Act of Preaching," in *Preaching as a Social Act: Theory and Practice,* ed. Arthur Van Seters (Nashville: Abingdon Press, 1988), 55–94; Leonora Tubbs Tisdale, *Preaching as Local Theology and Folk Art,* Fortress Resources for Preaching (Minneapolis: Fortress Press, 1997); Nancy T. Ammerman, Jackson W. Carroll, Carl S. Dudley, and William McKinney, eds., *Studying Congregations: A New Handbook* (Nashville: Abingdon Press, 1998); Thomas E. Frank, *The Soul of the Congregation* (Nashville: Abingdon Press, 2000); James R. Neiman and Thomas G. Rogers, *Preaching to Every Pew: Cross Cultural Strategies* (Minneapolis: Fortress Press, 2001).

⁷For an exploration of how sermons fit into congregational systems, see Ronald J. Allen, *Preaching and Practical Ministry,* Preaching and Its Partners (St. Louis: Chalice Press, 2001).

⁸Several interviewees lament that visiting preachers often overlook the local congregational context. For example, "We've had some visiting people who've come through who have been big, big name people. People who have been on television and people that somebody would come to hear because of that. I've been sometimes very, very turned off...I've seen people who've come in who have read their sermons, who you know have given them a thousand times but they just pulled it [the sermon they gave here] out of one that they had that at some point in time was fresh and wonderful, but I felt like it really wasn't fresh for us."

⁹For an excellent exploration of how preaching shapes congregational culture theologically and pastorally, see G. Lee Ramsey, Jr., *Care-Full Preaching: From Sermon to Caring Community* (St. Louis: Chalice Press, 2000).

¹⁰In subsequent chapters, we will note that for some other listeners, the integrity of the preacher has less effect upon their receptivity to the sermon.

¹¹This listener points to an important pastoral implication of this sermon that was never directly stated. "All of us have been touched by the death of a loved one. The pastor handled it [in this situation] in such a fashion that the pastor doesn't put somebody behind the pulpit to give their lesson. The pastor does it in such a fashion that I think it is not only comforting to someone who is giving a testimony about something that is highly personal and traumatic, but in this way he not only comforts them but *I think sends that message to us that we're never going through things alone. That should something like that happen to us, the pastor is sitting right there with us through it"* (my emphasis).

¹² Henry H. Mitchell points out that many sermons in African American congregations end with a celebration, that is, a time when the minister and congregation rejoice in the divine presence and leading in celebratory tones and movements. Celebration can occur earlier in the sermon, of course, but is usually most intense and long lasting in the last quarter of the sermon. See Henry H. Mitchell, *Black Preaching: The Recovery of a Powerful Art* (Nashville: Abingdon Press, 1990) and Frank A. Thomas, *They Like to Never Quit Praisin' God: The Role of Celebration in Preaching* (Cleveland: United Church Press, 1990).

Chapter 3: Logos Settings

¹Aristotle, *The "Art" of Rhetoric,* tr. John Henry Freese, Loeb Classical Library 23 (Cambridge: Harvard University Press, 1932), 17 (1.2.4–6).

²Lind Hogan and Robert S. Reid, *Connecting with the Congregation: Rhetoric and the Art of Preaching* (Nashville: Abingdon Press, 1999), 91.

³For a criticism of reducing logos to logic, see David Cunningham, *Faithful Persuasion: In Aid of a Rhetoric of Christian Theology* (Notre Dame, Ind.: University of Notre Dame Press, 1990), 157–64.

⁴Though Aristotle did not discuss imagination extensively in his major work on rhetoric, it is implied in *The Poetics,* tr. W. Hamilton Fyfe, The Loeb Classical Library (Cambridge:

Harvard University Press, 1932), vol. 23, 3–120. For an important study of sermons as imaginative experience, see Robert Reid, Jeffrey Bullock, and David Fleer, "Preaching as the Creation of an Experience: The Not-So-Rational Revolution of the New Homiletic," *The Journal of Communication and Religion* 18/1 (1995), 1–18.

[5]The fact that some listeners place so much value on the sermon (and so little on the rest of the service of worship) suggests that ministers and congregational leaders need to help congregations realize more fully the formative and interpretive power of the service of worship as a whole, and how the various parts of the life of the congregation can work together to help members of the community arrive at theologically satisfying interpretations of life. See, for instance, Ronald J. Allen, *Preaching and Practical Ministry.* Preaching and Its Partners (St. Louis: Chalice Press, 2001); Clark M. Williamson and Ronald J. Allen, *Adventures of the Spirit: The Service of Worship from the Perspective of Process Theology* (Lanham, Md. : University Press of America , 1997); idem, *The Vital Congregation* (St. Louis: Chalice Press, 1998).

[6]Hearing such statements of the high value of preaching from members of churches whose worship is typically centered in the word (and is not weekly word and table) is hardly surprising. However, half of the statements cited in this paragraph are from persons who belong to congregations who worship in high liturgical style and/or where the loaf is broken weekly.

[7]Few people in the study group—even from the high liturgical churches—commented that the sermon tied into the main themes set by the liturgy.

[8]In the survey data, we also find some listeners who approach the sermon through logos settings who prefer for the preacher not to make clear what they should take away from the sermon. They want to know what to think and they trust the preacher to help them. Like the critical spirit, which is highlighted in this part of the chapter, the preference for the preacher to speak straightforwardly is found in listeners in congregations who are located along the theological spectrum from liberal to conservative. The difference between people who appreciate critical evaluation in the sermon and those who prefer more directive preaching could be explained by faith development theory that notices that people operate with different modes of mental process. Directive preaching would be preferred by persons with synthetic-conventional faith (stage 3) while persons who appreciate comparison and contrast is consistent with individuating-reflective faith (stage 4). For an interpretation on faith development theory and its relationship to preaching, see Joseph R. Jeter, Jr. and Ronald J. Allen, *One Gospel, Many Ears: Preaching For Different Listeners in the Congregation* (St. Louis: Chalice Press, 2002), 51–61. In our study group, more people who listen on logos settings demonstrate characteristics of individuating-reflective faith.

[9]It is difficult for analysts to know the degree to which these statements are true. Persons trained in the psychological disciplines might say that some of the people who profess to be unemotional are not aware of (or do not acknowledge) the roles that feelings play. However, we are obliged to report these self-understandings.

[10]The inability to recall a specific sermon is not unusual. Most people in the study had difficulty remembering particular sermons (when asked to do so). However, this listener is not simply drawing a blank when asked to think of a response to a sermon to use as an example. This listener seems unaware that some sermons in the present congregation have drawn emotional responses.

Chapter 4: Pathos Settings

[1]As noted earlier, about twenty percent of the people interviewed for this study listen to the sermon through pathos settings, about forty percent each through ethos and logos settings.

[2]Aristotle, *The "Art" of Rhetoric,* tr. John Henry Freese, Loeb Classical Library 23 (Cambridge: Harvard University Press, 1932), 17 (1.2.4).

[3]For a trenchant discussion of pathos as "not only emotions, but also the wide variety of ways in which the state or condition of the audience affects the persuasive appeal of the speech," see David Cunningham, *Faithful Persuasion: In Aid of a Rhetoric of Christian Theology* (Notre Dame, Ind.: University of Notre Dame Press, 1990), 42–97. Our research focuses more narrowly on pathos as feeling.

[4]Lucy Lind Hogan and Robert Reid, *Connecting with the Congregation: Rhetoric and the Art of Preaching* (Nashville: Abingdon Press, 1999), 83.

⁵Ibid., 75.

⁶The classic discussion of identification is Kenneth Burke, *A Rhetoric of Motives* (Berkeley: University of California, 1950), 19–46. Identification, of course, also involves elements of ethos and logos. Lind Hogan and Reid discuss identification under the rubric of pathos in their *Connecting with the Congregation,* 78–79.

⁷More congregants who listen to the sermon on pathos settings speak of the importance to them of music in worship than do persons who hear through ethos and logos settings. The kinds of music that particular listeners find appealing stir the emotions in a direct and often powerful way. By contrast, a couple of persons who enter the sermon through logos settings prefer the "early service" which is conducted with no (or minimal) music because the quiet allows them to focus more intently.

⁸One cannot simply assume that a person listens to a sermon on pathos settings when a person says, "I am emotional." The latter conclusion comes only when the transcript reveals patterns of perception with a pathos character. Nor can one assume that a statement beginning with (or including) words such as "I feel..." is a pathos statement. Some people (including folk who hear the sermon through logos and ethos settings) use the expressions "I feel" and "feelings" (and related expressions) when they mean "I think" and "thoughts" or "ideas."

⁹A minister taking this route must use discretion in regard to the stories that the preacher might want to bring into the sermon. For guidance in the use of personal material in preaching, see Richard Thulin, *The "I" of the Sermon: Autobiography in the Pulpit,* Fortress Resources for Preaching (Minneapolis: Fortress Press, 1989).

¹⁰Whether or not the preacher intends for a story to stir the life of feeling, a story may do so. Even when a preacher tells a story for a utilitarian purpose, the story may have evocative power to move the listening at deep levels. Hence, a preacher should examine every story in the sermon to determine the likely associations it will call forth and to assess whether these associations are consistent with the gospel.

¹¹The number of people who speak of God being active in the sermon is about the same in all three groups—ethos, logos, and pathos. The distinctive element among parishioners who audit sermons on pathos settings is that they speak of God and the Holy Spirit working, specifically, through feeling. Surprisingly, the number of extended references to the presence and activity of Jesus Christ is rather small and is not associated with any one group.

¹²If the preacher does not agree theologically that the Holy Spirit can move through feeling, the preacher, needs to explain why.

¹³For reflections on the relationship between preaching and pastoral care, see G. Lee Ramsey, Jr., *Care-full Preaching: From Sermon to Caring Community* (St. Louis: Chalice Press, 2000).

Chapter 5: Three Settings and One Sermon

¹Different denominations, as well as less formal Christian collaborations and theological movements, express different theological norms. For a compact consideration of the theological purposes of preaching in eleven historic Christian movements, see Ronald J. Allen, *Believing Is Preaching: The Sermon as Theological Reflection* (Louisville: Westminster John Knox Press, 2002), 129–41; and idem., *Interpreting the Gospel: An Introduction to Preaching* (St. Louis: Chalice Press, 1998), 24–28, 73–80. The criteria that I use (derived from Clark M. Williamson and discussed in the preceding books) are (1) appropriateness to the gospel, (2) intelligibility, and (3) moral plausibility. Burton Z Cooper and John S. McClure, *Claiming Theology in the Pulpit* (Louisville: Westminster John Knox Press, 2003) offer a user-friendly theological profile that helps preachers identify the theology that they actually preach (which is sometimes different from the theological viewpoints to which they are committed) as well as practical suggestions for helping preachers reinforce or move towards preaching theology to which they are committed and which they want to preach.

²My suspicion, based on informal conversations with pastors is that most preachers are much more restrained than they need to be, at least for persons with a strong ethos orientation to listening, in articulating their foundational theological convictions and how they most deeply believe the church is called to witness. Some preachers are so concerned not to offend that they take little advantage of the power of the ministerial office to call the congregation to mission or to accountability.

[3]Though none of the people in the sample made this connection, hearing the story of the preacher's struggle is also an opportunity to recognize that just as God was with the preacher through the struggle, so God is with the congregation. A caution that comes to mind, though it did not come to expression in any of the interviews, is that a listener's interest in the preacher's "reality" could easily drift into the voyeurism that is found in so many sectors of North American culture in which people are titillated by the private affairs of others or for no redeeming purpose, or even live vicariously through the experiences of others.

[4]On imitation, see Michael J. Wilkins, "Imitate, Imitators," *The Anchor Bible Dictionary,* ed. David Noel Freedman et al., vol. 3 (Garden City, N.Y. : Doubleday, 1992), 392.

[5]In so doing, the preacher might make the important theological point that God knows us individually and collectively by name, knows our circumstances, and loves and empowers us in our particularity.

[6]This suggestion applies to listeners across the theological spectrum–from those who have more liberal ways of interpreting the Bible to those who are more conservative in orientation. Only a few listeners in either group, or persons in between, manifest awareness of the best and deepest in their traditions' understandings of how to interpret the Bible in its historical setting or how to make use of it today. For the unsatisfactory character of the terms liberal and conservative, but recognizing the utility in their use, see Joseph R. Jeter, Jr. and Ronald J. Allen, *One Gospel, Many Ears: Preaching and Different Listeners in the Congregation* (St. Louis: Chalice Press, 2002), 149–74.

[7]Several quotations from interviewees cited in this book do.

[8]Manipulation is persuading people to follow a certain course of thought or action without recognizing other possible courses of action and without considering the relationship of the recommended thought or action to important values of the community.

[9]Preachers themselves are sometimes tempted to think of the sermon as an end in itself because of, as one of my former students said, "the incredible feeling that comes from holding a congregation in the palm of one's hand."

[10]A listener recalls a case when a preacher did use too many words. "[A certain minister] can on occasion spend quite a bit more time than is necessary or desirable in giving the details about a story. [This minister] preached a funeral for someone whom [the minister] did not know very well… To start out by talking about when [the minister] was [young], there was a very fancy car, an expensive, well-made car, fine finish, and all that type of thing, and how much [the minister] liked that car. The whole theme was that the [person] who died was really a kind of vintage model and we wouldn't see the likes of that person again. But I think [the minister] spent far too much getting the technique of saying something everyone could relate to. To grab your audience, that might be effective, but get it over with quickly."

[11]I cannot tell the degree to which this paucity is the result of the questions in the interviews (that did not prompt such reflection), self-absorption on the part of these listeners, or other factors.

[12]The questions asked in the study did not specifically probe one of the issues that has dominated much discussion in the preaching community for the last generation–the form or genre of the sermon. With respect to the form of the sermon, the study suggests that different forms may appeal to different people, and different kinds of material within the sermon make different kinds of contact with different kinds of people. An immediate implication is that ministers need to be able to preach in modes that are listener-friendly for persons on the different settings (as well as to include different kinds of material in sermons–logical argument, scientific data, personal testimony, images, poignant stories, etc. for the same reason). To reframe one of the listeners' comments, "One size does not fit all." No one approach to the form or genre of the sermon will do for every listener, congregation, or occasion. For a catalogue of thirty-four recent and historical ways of developing sermons, see Ronald J. Allen, *Patterns of Preaching: A Sermon Sampler* (St. Louis: Chalice Press, 1998).

[13]These possibilities are similar to the ones discussed in connection with preaching and other forms of diversity in the congregation (e.g., age, gender, patterns of mental operation, cultures, relationship to the congregation, theological viewpoints) in Jeter and Allen, *One Gospel, Many Ears,* 15–18.

[14]A similar table focused on different aspects of listening (age, modes of mental operation, gender, relationship to the congregation, theological orientation) is found in Jeter and Allen, *One Gospel, Many Ears,* 179–81.

[15]A preacher may consistently give disproportionate attention to certain settings while neglecting others in their sermons over time. A preacher, for instance, may continuously think of the sermon in terms of its emotional effect while not developing the content of the sermon with precision and depth. A chart similar to this one can help the preacher recognize over-emphasis and under-emphasis, and, therefore, to take corrective steps.

Chapter 6: An Example: A Sermon on Luke 3:7–18

[1]Since I teach full-time in a theological seminary, I do not serve a congregation. My preaching is virtually always as a guest—a significant disadvantage in that one seldom has a thick understanding of congregational context.

[2]See further Ronald J. Allen, *Preaching Luke-Acts*, Preaching Classic Texts (St. Louis: Chalice Press, 2000). For a more technical and detailed exposition of the perspective on Luke-Acts assumed in this exegesis see Ronald J. Allen's essays in *Chalice Introduction to the New Testament*, ed. Dennis Smith (St. Louis: Chalice Press, 2004), "The Story of Jesus According to 'Luke': The Gospel of Luke" (pp. 175–97) and "The Story of the Church According to 'Luke': The Acts of the Apostles" (pp. 198–219).

[3]Allen, *Preaching Luke-Acts*, 123–39.

[4]A different possibility for understanding the situation of tax collectors and the soldiers in relationship to Luke's community is to think that the Lukan congregation may not have welcomed tax collectors and soldiers even when the latter had repented. If this is the case, we would interpret Luke as subtly reminding the community of their responsibility to be hospitable to tax collectors and soldiers.

[5]Even Luke's pictures of the results of not sharing as condemnation and fiery punishment (e.g., the foolish barn builder in Lk. 12:13–21, the rich person in Lk. 16:19–31, Ananias and Sapphira in Acts 5:1–11) are not angry outbursts but are pastoral invitations from Luke to those with resources to use their resources to provide abundant life for all and thereby to avoid condemnation.

[6]On the Spirit, see further Allen, *Preaching Luke-Acts*, 71–88.

[7]On the hermeneutic of analogy, see Stephen W. Farris, *Preaching that Matters: The Bible and Our Lives* (Louisville: Westminster John Knox Press, 1999).

[8]As a revisionary theologian in the process school of theology, I do not believe that, in a single apocalyptic cataclysm, God will end the present world, consign people to a fiery condemnation, and manifest the divine realm. However, as the sermon makes clear, I do think repentance is essential to creating a new social world and that it can help avoid the consequences of injustice, idolatry, and other forms of sin. On this theological perspective, see further John C. Holbert and Ronald J. Allen, *Holy Root, Holy Branches: Christian Preaching from the Old Testament* (Nashville: Abingdon Press, 1995), 123–28; Clark M. Williamson and Ronald J. Allen, *A Credible and Timely Word: Process Theology and Preaching* (St. Louis: Chalice Press, 1991), 105–11.

[9]For a discussion of ministry and systemic change, see Rufus Burrow, Jr., and Mary Alice Mulligan, *Daring to Speak for God: Ethical Prophecy in Ministry* (Cleveland: Pilgrim Press, 2002).

[10]In a number of other congregations, I have found that some people expect a professor (at least this professor) in the pulpit to be tedious and esoteric and even to come across with "an air of superiority." Consequently, I try to use language and material (especially light humor, when appropriate) that is accessible and interesting without watering down the content. I also sought to avoid the danger of drifting into self-righteousness and judgmentalism that is so easy when preaching on prophetic texts.

[11]In some sermons I tell stories from my own life experience, but I could not think of such a story from my own experience that fit this sermon. Had I done so, I would have followed the advice of several interviewees and told a story that depicted how I am in solidarity with the congregation as a person in need of God's grace or as a comrade in struggle (rather than using myself as a hero or model).

[12]Here we are reminded that settings persistently interact with one another. The suggestion that the preacher can help people who feel confused by the text's belief that the apocalypse is on the immediate horizon by naming the confusion and offering an alternative is, of course, a logos response to a phenomenon that includes a significant pathos dimension. I would point out, then, that the feeling of confusion is at least partly caused by logos—the text asking

the reader to believe something that is (for some listeners) hard to believe. As a preacher, I hope that clarification of belief can help with resolving feelings.

[13]A preacher may sometimes create a story to serve the purposes of a particular sermon. When a preacher makes up a story, it is important to signal that fact to the congregation so as not to leave the impression that the sermon is reporting an event that actually occurred. The preacher's integrity is on the line.

[14]Collect for the Third Sunday in Advent, *The Book of Common Prayer* (New York: The Church Hymnal Corporation and Seabury Press, 1977), 212.

Appendices

[1]For samples of transcripts of complete interviews, see John S. McClure, Ronald J. Allen, Dale P. Andrews, L. Susan Bond, Dan P. Moseley, and G. Lee Ramsey, Jr., *Listening to Listeners: Homiletical Case Studies* (St. Louis: Chalice Press, 2004).

[2]As noted in chapter 2, discussions of ethos in rhetoric increasingly think of ethos as having two dimensions. Internal ethos refers to qualities that the listener perceives in the preacher (or other speaker) in the sermon event itself that the listener takes to mean that the preacher is trustworthy. External ethos refers to qualities of the preacher outside the sermon event (e.g., in pastoral calling or church administration) that the listener interprets as meaning that the preacher is trustworthy. See Lucy Lind Hogan and Robert Reid, *Connecting with the Congregation: Rhetoric and the Art of Preaching* (Nashville: Abingdon Press, 1999), 53–65. Cf. David S. Cunningham, *Faithful Persuasion: In Aid of a Rhetoric of Christian Theology* (Notre Dame, Ind.: University of Notre Dame Press, 1990), 100–147. In chapter 2, we call attention to a permutation in understanding ethos that we call congregational culture. Congregational culture (which is related to external ethos but is a category not found in traditional rhetoric) refers to how the perception of the preacher by the *congregation as community* is affected by, and affects, the willingness of the congregation to receive the sermon. Ethos typically refers to the more conventional rhetorical understanding of ethos as the perception by an individual listener of the character and trustworthiness of the preacher that prompts the listener to regard the preacher as more (or less) worthy of confidence. Scholars of rhetoric could argue that what we call congregational culture is not excluded by the traditional designations, especially external ethos. However, the interviews place such a powerful emphasis on the perception of the preacher as a part of local congregational culture that we believe this culture deserves its own place in discussion. Questions 1–7 probe congregational culture while questions 8 and 9 explore traditional ethos. John S. McClure et al., *Listening to Listeners*, 8–9, discuss more fully the nuances we give to the ethos category.

[3]An analyst needs to pay careful attention to how *each listener* specifically uses language, and not simply assume that the presence of a certain word signals that listener's orientation. For example, as noted earlier, the expression "I feel" is typically associated with the pathos setting. However, occasional persons on the logos setting use the words "I feel" as a synonym for "I think."

[4]These expressions are typically part of the semantic field associated with each setting.

Printed in the United States
76250LV00004B/166

9 780827 205017